IN THE TWILIGHT

OF

WESTERN THOUGHT

*Studies in the Pretended Autonomy
of Philosophical Thought*

Herman Dooyeweerd

THE CRAIG PRESS
Nutley, New Jersey
1972

UNIVERSITY SERIES, Philosophical Studies
Dr. Gordon H. Clark, Editor

LIBRARY OF CONGRESS CATALOG CARD NUMBER LC 60-6645

Printed in the United States of America

IN THE TWILIGHT
OF WESTERN THOUGHT

Contents

Introduction   *vii*

  I. *The Pretended Autonomy of Philo-*
     sophical Thought—I   *1*

  II. *The Pretended Autonomy of Philo-*
     sophical Thought—II   *27*

  III. *The Sense of History and the Histori-*
     cal World and Life View—I   *61*

  IV. *The Sense of History and the Histori-*
     cal World and Life View—II   *83*

  V. *Philosophy and Theology—I*   *113*

  VI. *Philosophy and Theology—II*   *132*

  VII. *Philosophy and Theology—III*   *157*

  VIII. *What is Man?*   *173*

  The Author   *197*

Introduction

The lectures in this book are Dooyeweerd's own introduction to his philosophy and an excellent guide to the study of his recently translated *A New Critique of Theoretical Thought* (4 vols.).[1] Again, J. M. Spier's two studies, *What is Calvinistic Philosophy?*,[2] and especially *An Introduction to Christian Philosophy*,[1] provide a valuable analysis of Dooyeweerd's thinking. Our purpose therefore will not be a review of his already ably surveyed thought but an analysis of its general significance.

Dooyeweerd would be the first to disclaim originality, or that his is a final system, but rather declares that his is a development of Christian philosophy on the biblical foundations of John Calvin and Abraham Kuyper. As such, his philosophy is of major importance and of far-reaching implications.

Central to Dooyeweerd's position is the insistence that truly Christian philosophy can alone be critical, and that non-Christian philosophy is inevitably dogmatical. Basic to all non-Christian philosophies are certain far-reaching pre-theoretical commitments or

[2] Wm. B. Erdmans Publishing Co. (Grand Rapids).
[1] Presbyterian and Reformed Publishing Co. (Philadelphia).

presuppositions which are basically religious. Man assumes the self-sufficiency and autonomy of his philosophical thought. He makes God relative, and his thought, or some aspect of creation, absolute. As a result of this attitude, man, in his pretended autonomy, immediately finds that, not only is the world of everyday experience a problem, but that he is a problem to himself. Wherever man has, in terms of this presupposition, tried to think philosophically, he has found it all too easy, whether in China or in the West, to end up in skepticism even concerning his own existence, or at least of his thinking processes. As a result, he finds himself often caught between the tension of radical doubt and an acceptance of all perception as substantial because the perceiving subject, man, in his thinking is himself substance, i. e., being that subsists in itself. This is the paradox so ably set forth in Hume in part and clearly in Kant. Substance ceased to be metaphysical for Kant and became epistemological, a form or category of thought. A similar paradox seems to have existed in the philosophy of Metrodorus of Chios, a fourth century B.C. Greek skeptic, who could affirm these two things:

1. "None of us knows anything, not even whether we know or do not know, nor do we know whether not knowing and knowing exist, nor in general whether there is anything or not.
2. Everything exists which anyone perceives."[1]

Here is a hapless Scylla and Charybdis with no middle

[1] Kathleen Freeman: *Ancilla to the Pre-Socratic Philosophies,* Harvard, 1957, p. 120 f.

course. As a result of this dogmatic character of non-Christian philosophy, the naive experience of reality becomes a problem, and the men of philosophy become darker than children in their light. Philosophy must resort to antinomies and paradoxes, because its basically religious faith is apostate faith and hence with no law or norm beyond itself or some aspect of creation. It cannot absolutize any aspect of that created order, which has meaning because created and sustained by God, without obscuring or destroying meaning, and also creating insoluble tensions in that order. Dooyeweerd has in particular analyzed the hapless tensions of Hellenic, medieval, and humanist cultures, as against the presuppositions of truly Christian culture, the fundamental motives of cultures being in essense religious and a product of the basic pre-theoretical commitments of man. The tensions of each culture are regarded as basic tensions of life itself by the members of that culture, because they assume to be ultimate that which is actually a religious condition and ground of their own thought. Each culture, however, is a product of its philosophy, and its philosophy is the expression of its religious presuppositions. The philosophy and the religious presuppositions may change in form, but basic to all non-Christian cultures is the dogma of the autonomy of theoretical thought and its ostensibly critical and non-religious character. It is this dogma which Dooyeweerd so thoroughly challenges and exposes, while delineating the framework of Christian philosophy and culture. In doing this, he is, as Cornelius

Van Til has pointed out, "as unashamed as was Calvin in his insistence that man's pre-theoretical commitments determine his outlook in philosophy."[2]

Dooyeweerd, together with Vollenhoven, has developed the Philosophy of the *Wetsidee,* of the Cosmonomic-Idea. It is impossible, Dooyeweerd holds, to argue across systems, because each can "prove" the error of the other in terms of its basic presuppositions. These basic presuppositions are by no means philosophic but are "self-evident" prejudices of a religious nature. These religious dogmas are assumed to be axioms of thought and remain unexamined and undetected because the non-Christian has no vantage from which to be critical of philosophy; he has no Archimedean point within creation. Dooyeweerd, on the other hand, by beginning with the biblical presuppositions, is able, because the cosmos is in all of its aspects ordered by law instituted by the Creator-Redeemer, to be critical in a way non-Christian philosophy cannot be.

What is the outcome of this approach to philosophy and culture? Non-Christian philosophy and culture by its very nature, tends inevitably to tension, paradox and antinomy. It cannot do justice to naive experience and inevitably emasculates both life and thought. Two examples of this will suffice.

First, let us consider the implications of Joseph Haroutunian's *Lust For Power.* For Haroutunian, power is a dangerous thing, and man's desire for

---

[2] C. Van Til in *The Westminster Theological Journal,* May, 1955 XVII, 2, p. 182 f.

power is "the prime unreason in human life and bedevils the whole existence of man." It is a product of the "despair of being" and is thus a substitute for life and yet as a condition of life "becomes more valuable than life."

> "No amount of power can change being's being in relation to nonbeing, or remove the dread in human existence. Power rather establishes dread and much power turns it into a panic. This is why the more powerful men are, the more dangerous they are. This is why men of power are exposed to arbitrary and irrational action which lets loose torrents of devastating evil. There is no telling when they will make a 'mistake' which will mean wholesale misery and even death. Great men or men of power are men who are 'at their rope's end.' Power is the last substitute for life which can be proposed in this world."[3]

Power is seen as opposed to and a substitute for love. "A man isolated from his fellowmen seeks mastery over them as the best means of security and contentment. He hopes to do with power what he has failed to do without love." "Love for life is the only authentic antidote to lust in general and to lust for power in particular."[4] It is apparent that Haroutunian sees power only as an evil, and as opposed to love, never as an aspect of the divine image in man. Dooyeweerd, in his second lecture on "The Sense of History," comments, "Even the most terrible misuse of cultural power in our sinful world cannot make

[3] Joseph Haroutunian, *Lust for Power*, Scribner's, New York, 1949 pp. 74-76.
[4] *Ibid.*, pp. 38, 140.

power itself sinful, nor can it detract from the normative sense of man's cultural vocation." If a fallen world is the source of norms, then inevitably an emasculating tension results; love is opposed to power, nature to freedom, or nature to grace, matter to form, and so on. To absolutize one aspect of creation is to distort all of creation and render it void of meaning. As modern man attempts to empty God and man of power, he empties love of power and meaning also. Karl Barth declares, "God and 'power in itself' are mutually exclusive. God is the essence of the possible; but 'power in itself' is the essence of the impossible."[5] By making God "the essence of the possible," that is, with unrealized potentialities, he also makes God destructive of every possible norm. Similarly, according to Plutarch, the Temple of Isis at Sais bore this inscription of the deity's statement: "I am all that has come into being, and that which is, and that which shall be; and no man hath lifted my veil." In terms of this, God is not an everlasting being but an ever-becoming, non-personal and identifiable with the cosmos and its process. In sharp opposition to this, as John presented the divine norm to the church, he identified God as He "which is, and which was, and which is to come" (Revelation 1:4), that is, as the eternal one who manifests Himself in history, and, as creator, redeemer and judge, "is to come." Only such a God can provide man with a true cultural vocation and a norm whereby he is able to be critical

[5] Karl Barth: *Dogmatics in Outline.* 1949, Philosophical Library, New York, p. 48.

and constructive. The Christian man, faithful to this norm, can do justice to his experience and his vocation, whereas the non-Christian emasculates himself and his world as the necessary consequence of his immanence-standpoint.

Second, let us examine Rudolf Bultmann on science. In his de-mythologizing, Bultmann openly avows that "the modern world-view" is his criterion. He recognizes that the *results* of science vary from age to age, but asserts the *principles* to be permanent, and hence to be man's guide rather than the mythological which he sees in Scripture. Thus, having made science the source of "permanent principles," Bultmann has apparently found a new source of norms, one within the cosmos. Actually, however, having made the relative absolute, he finds it also become demonic. Science now becomes the source of "man-made security." "The scientific world-view engenders a great temptation, namely, that man strive for mastery over the world and over his own life."[6] "Science now becomes the builder of countless towers of Babel which history must destroy, and is the implicit source of the demonic."[7] There follows then the necessity that "In faith I realize that the scientific world-view does not comprehend the whole reality of the world and of human life, but faith does not offer another general world-view which corrects science in its statements on its own level. Rather faith acknowl-

[6] Rudolf Bultmann: *Jesus Christ and Mythology*, Scribner's 1958, pp. 35-39.
[7] *Ibid.*, pp. 39, 40, 42.

edges that the world-view given by science is a necessary means for doing our work within the world."[8] As a vantage point of defense and perspective against this scientific juggernaut, Bultmann finds "genuine freedom" only in "freedom from the motivation of the moment," that is, history and the cosmos, and this is only possible in "a law which has its origin and reason in the beyond . . . . the law of God."[9] And yet, because God cannot act, and the only permanent principles are from science, which is itself now the source of the demonic, security is impossible, and "He who abandons every form of security shall find true security." De-mythologizing is equated with justification as the means of salvation, because it destroys every longing for security.[10] Salvation is thus a permanent state of anxiety and neurosis, and the world a profane place.

Here indeed is an emasculation of life, science, history and law. Bultmann begins by deifying science as the source of permanent principles and ends by regarding it as the great temptation to a false security, as the source in effect of the demonic. Dooyeweerd begins by denying that science is the source of permanent principles and ends by establishing scientific activity as a part of man's vocation and calling. In terms of the divine image he bears, man is called to exercise, among other things, knowledge and dominion in the scientific spheres by subduing the

[8] *Ibid.*, p. 65.
[9] *Ibid.*, p. 41.
[10] *Ibid.*, p. 84.

earth. Science is an aspect of his divine vocation in a world of law and a legitimate area of holy activity. The view thus which seemingly "rejects" science becomes the only source of true science, whereas any view which makes absolute that which is relative ends up by destroying the value of that aspect of creation and emasculating life and experience. The cultural and historical, as well as philosophical, implications of Dooyeweerd's position are thus far-reaching.[11] Here is a philosophy with universality and power. Its extensive influence already in Europe is thus not to be wondered at.

Two minor points may be noted. Dooyeweerd has been criticized for using the word *motive* instead of *motif*. Let us note, however, the difference between these two words. Motive means 1) that which incites to motive or action; 2) a predominant idea; design. Motif means the leading feature in literary or artistic work, especially in music. Motif implies a conscious and deliberate pattern. Motive implies exactly what Dooyeweerd is concerned with, the religious presuppositions of a culture, the ground of thought rather than the product of thought, as with motif.

Again, the criticism of certain aspects of Dooyeweerd's philosophy have been used as an excuse to evade the force of the whole. But Dooyeweerd, no more than Calvin and Kuyper before him, has arrived at a final formulation or is free from occasional defects

[11] An excellent application of one aspect of this philosophy is to be found in H. Van Riessen: *The Society of the Future* (Presbyterian and Reformed Publishing Co.) .

or inconsistencies. These, however, surely need to be noted, but cannot be used as an excuse to evade the main thrust of his philosophy which has not been met or successfully challenged. It gives important and exciting direction to present and future thought and action and is, in the fullest sense of the word, a Christian philosophy and a great one.

Rousas John Rushdoony
Santa Cruz, Calif.

January 1960

IN THE TWILIGHT
OF WESTERN THOUGHT

The Pretended Autonomy
of Philosophical Thought—I

Every philosophy which claims a Christian starting-point is confronted with the traditional dogma concerning the autonomy of philosophical thought, implying its independence of all religious presuppositions. It may be posited that this dogma is the only one that has survived the general decay of the earlier certitudes in philosophy. This decay was caused by the fundamental spiritual uprooting of Western thought since the two world wars.

Nevertheless, it is the very crisis in the earlier fundamentals of philosophical thought, which has paved the way for a radical criticism of the dogma of autonomy. Such a criticism is not only necessary from a Christian point of view, much rather it must be considered the primary condition of a truly critical attitude of thought in every kind of philosophical reflection, irrespective of the difference in starting-point. For the acceptance of the autonomy of theoretical thought has been elevated to an intrinsic condition of true philosophy without its having been

1

justified by a critical inquiry into the inner structure of the theoretical attitude of thought itself.

So long as the belief in human theoretical reason as the ultimate judge in matters of truth and falsehood was unchallenged, this belief could be accepted as a theoretical axiom. But it is this very belief, which, to a high degree, has been undermined in our day as a result of a radical historicism, the influence of depth-psychology, the so-called *Lebensphilosophie* and, at least in Europe, the powerful influence of Existentialism. This makes the assertion that autonomy is the primary condition of philosophical thought all the more problematic, insofar as it is maintained in the present situation of Western philosophy.

But apart from the present crisis of all former certitudes, there are other reasons for making the dogma, concerning the autonomy of philosophical thought, into a critical problem. In the first place, this pretended autonomy, which is considered the common basis of ancient Greek, Thomistic scholastic and modern secularized philosophy, lacks that unity of meaning necessary for such a common foundation. In Greek philosophy it had a meaning quite different from that in Thomistic scholasticism. In both of them it was conceived in a sense quite different from that which it assumed in modern secularized thought. As soon as we seek to penetrate to the root of these fundamentally different conceptions, we are confronted with a fundamental difference in presuppositions which surpasses the boundaries of theoretical thought.

In the last analysis these very presuppositions determine the meaning ascribed to this autonomy. This does not agree with the traditional dogmatic view of philosophical thought. For this view implies that the ultimate starting-point of philosophy should be found in this thought itself. But due to the lack of a univocal sense, the pretended autonomy cannot guarantee a common basis to the different philosophical trends. On the contrary, it appears again and again that this dogma impedes a real contact between philosophical schools and trends that prove to differ in their deepest, supra-theoretical presuppositions. This is the second reason why we can no longer accept it as an axiom which simply gives expression to an intrinsical condition of true philosophy.

If all philosophical currents that pretend to choose their starting-point in theoretical reason alone, had, indeed, no deeper presuppositions, it should be possible to settle every philosophical argument between them in a purely theoretical way. But the factual situation is quite different. A debate between philosophical trends which are fundamentally opposed to each other usually results in a reasoning at cross-purposes, because they are not able to find a way to penetrate to each other's true starting-points. The latter seem to be masked by the dogma concerning the autonomy of philosophical thought. And as long as there exists a fundamental difference in the philosophical views of meaning and experience, it does not help if, in line with contemporary logical positivism and linguistic analysis, we seek to establish criteria for meaningful and meaningless philosophical propositions and require their verifiability.

It may be granted that this factual situation does not yet prove the impossibility of an autonomous philosophical theory which lacks any presupposition of a supra-rational character. But it is, in any case, sufficient to show that it is necessary to make the dogmatical assertions concerning the autonomy of theoretical thought into a *critical problem*.

This problem should be posed as a *questio iuris*. This means that in the last analysis we are not concerned with the question as to whether philosophical thought in its *factual* development has displayed an autonomous character making it independent of belief and religion. Much rather, the question at issue is whether this autonomy is required by the inner nature of thought, and thus is implied in this nature as an intrinsic possibility.

This question can only be answered by a transcendental criticism of the theoretical attitude of thought as such. By this we understand a radically critical inquiry into the universally valid conditions which alone make theoretical thought possible, and which are required by the inner structure and nature of this thought itself.

This latter restriction shows the fundamental difference between a transcendent and a transcendental critique of philosophical thought. A transcendent critique has nothing to do with the inner structure of the theoretical attitude of philosophical thinking and its necessary conditions. Much rather it criticizes the results of a philosophical reflection from a viewpoint which lies beyond the philosophical point of view. A theologian, for instance, may criticize the Kantian view of autonomous morality from the viewpoint of the Christian faith. But this critique remains dogmatic and worthless from the philosophical viewpoint so long as the inner point of connection between Christian faith and philosophy remains in the dark and the autonomy of philosophical thought is granted as an axiom. Theology itself is in need of a transcendental critique of theoretical thought, since it is bound to the theoretical attitude and always has philosophical presuppositions.

Philosophy, on the other hand, is in need of this criticism since it is the only way to conquer a theoretical dogmatism which lacks a radical self-critique. Under the influence of the dogmatical acceptance of the autonomy of philosophical thought such a radical critique was excluded up to now. Neither Kant, the founder of the so-called critical transcendental philosophy, nor Edmund Husserl, the founder of modern phenomenology, who called his phenomenological philosophy the most radical critique of knowledge, have made the theoretical attitude of thought into a critical problem. Both of them started from the autonomy of theoretical thinking as an axiom which needs no further justification. This is the dogmatical presupposition of their theoretical inquiry which makes the critical character of the latter problematic and masks their real starting-point, which, as a matter of fact, rules their manner of positing the philosophical problems.

We do not demand that the adherents of this dogma abandon it by anticipation. We only ask them to abstain from the dogmatical assertion that it is a necessary condition of any true philosophy and to subject this assertion to the test of a transcendental critique of theoretical thought itself.

How is the theoretical attitude of thought characterized? What is its inner structure by which it differs from the non-theoretical attitude of thinking? It displays an antithetic structure wherein the logical aspect of our thought is opposed to the non-logical aspects of our temporal experience. To comprehend this antithetical relation it is necessary to consider that our theoretical thought is bound to the temporal horizon of human experience and moves within this horizon. Within the temporal order, this experience displays a great diversity of fundamental modal aspects, or modalities which in the first place are aspects of time itself. These aspects do not, as such, refer to a concrete *what,* i. e., to concrete things or events, but only to the *how,* i. e., the particular and fundamental mode, or manner, in which we experience them. Therefore we speak of the modal aspects of this experience to underline that they are only the fundamental *modes* of the latter. They should not be identified with the concrete phenomena of empirical reality, which function, in principle, in all of these aspects. Which, then, are these fundamental modes of our experience? I shall enumerate them briefly.

Our temporal empirical horizon has a numerical *modes of experience .* aspect, a spatial aspect, an aspect of extensive movement, an aspect of energy in which we experience the physico-chemical relations of empirical reality, a biotic aspect, or that of organic life, an aspect of feeling and sensation, a logical aspect, i. e., the analytical manner of distinction in our temporal experience which lies at the foundation of all our concepts and logical judgments. Then there is a historical aspect in which we experience the cultural manner of development of our societal life. This is followed by the aspect of symbolical signification, lying at the foundation of all empirical linguistic phenomena. Furthermore there is the aspect of social intercourse, with its rules of courtesy, politeness, good breeding, fashion, and so forth. This experiential mode is followed by the economic, aesthetic, juridical and moral aspects, and, finally, by the aspect of faith or belief.

This whole diversity of modal aspects of our experience makes sense only within the order of time. It refers to a supra-temporal, central unity and fulness *proof ?* of meaning in our experiential world, which is refracted in the order of time into a rich diversity of modi, or modalities of meaning, just as sun-light is refracted by a prism in a rich diversity of colors. A simple reflection may make this clear. In the order of time, human existence and experience display a great diversity of modal aspects, but this diversity is *diversity & the self (unity)* related to the central unity of the human selfhood, which, as such, surpasses all modal diversity of our temporal experience. In the order of time the divine law for creation displays a great diversity of modalities. But this whole modal diversity of laws is related to the central unity of the divine law, namely, the commandment to love God and our neighbor.

However, in the theoretical attitude of thought we oppose the logical aspect of our thinking and experience to the non-logical modalities in order to acquire an analytical insight into the latter. These non-logical aspects, however, offer resistance to our attempt to grasp them in a logical concept and this resistance gives rise to theoretical problems. Such theoretical problems are, for example, What is the modal meaning of number? of space? of organic life? of cultural history? of economy? of law? of faith? And these problems are of a philosophical character since they refer to the fundamental modi of human experience, which lie at the foundation of all our concrete experience of diversity in things, events, and so forth.

It is true that in principle the different modal aspects delimit also the special viewpoints under which the different branches of empirical science examine the empirical world. This merely corroborates our view concerning the modal diversity of our experiential horizon and our view of theoretical thought in general. But these special sciences do not direct their attention upon the inner nature and structure of these modal aspects as such, but rather upon the variable phenomena which function in them in a special manner. The inner nature and structure of the special modal aspects which delimit their field of research is a presupposition of every special science.

It is only philosophy which can make this presupposition into a theoretical problem. For it is impossible to conceive the special meaning and inner structure of a modal aspect without having a philosophical insight into the whole temporal coherence of all the different modal aspects of our temporal horizon of experience. The reason is that every aspect can unfold its proper modal meaning only in this total coherence which expresses itself in its own inner structure. This is why this modal structure displays a great diversity of components, or moments, which in turn unfold the modal meaning of the aspect concerned only in their total coherence.

In the first place, every experiential aspect, or mode of experience, has a modal kernel which guarantees its irreducible, special meaning. But this modal kernel of its meaning can only express itself in a series of so-called analogical moments referring to the modal kernels of all the other aspects of our experience which precede or succeed, respectively, the aspect concerned in the temporal order. In accordance with the different direction of their reference, they may be distinguished into retrospective and anticipatory moments. Viewed in themselves these analogical moments are multivocal since they occur also in the other experiential aspects wherein, however, they display a different meaning. Their proper modal sense is only determined by the modal kernel of the aspect in whose structure they function. Nevertheless, they maintain their coherence with the aspects to which they refer.

Let us take, for example, the sensitive aspect of our

experience. Its modal kernel is that irreducible moment of feeling which cannot be defined in a logical way. *"Was man nicht definieren kann, das sicht man als ein Fuhlen an."* But this German adage is applicable to the modal kernel of each aspect. The nuclear moment of feeling, however, unfolds its modal sense only in an unbreakable coherence with a whole series of analogical moments, referring backward to earlier arranged aspects of our experience. Feeling has its own mode of life, bound to the aspect of organic life by its sensory moment. It is emotional, and emotion is a sensitive and intensive mode of movement, referring backward to the modal kernel of the original aspect of extensive movement. It has its own mode of energy or force, with grades of intensity, its causes and effects, by which it manifests its coherence with the physico-chemical aspect. It manifests its coherence with the spatial aspect in spatial analogies, namely, the subjective sensation of spatiality and the objective sensory space of our sensory perception, whose modal meaning is quite different from that of pure mathematical space, physical space, biotic space, and so forth.

All these structural moments of the sensitive aspect are also present in more developed animal feeling. But in the human experience this aspect unfolds also structural moments of an anticipatory character in which its coherence with the subsequently arranged aspects of our temporal horizon manifests itself. Feeling for logical coherence, historico-cultural feeling, linguistic feeling, aesthetic feeling, jural feeling, moral feeling, and so forth, are such anticipatory analogical moments in the modal structure of the sensitive aspect which deepen and open up, or disclose, its modal meaning.

Thus this modal structure reflects the whole coherence of the different aspects of our experience in a special modal sense. And the same holds good with respect to each other aspect, as I have shown in detail in the second volume of my work: *A New Critique of Theoretical Thought*. This may be called the universality of each experiential aspect within its own modal sphere.

As remarked, the theoretical problem concerning these modal structures of our experience is of a philosophical character. But a transcendental critique of philosophical thought is concerned with previous problems which are of a still more fundamental character.

The antithetical structure of the theoretical attitude of thought, gives rise to the question: Does this antithetical relation between the logical aspect and the non-logical aspects of our temporal experience correspond with the internal structure of the latter? The answer must be negative.

This theoretical antithesis originates only in our intention to conceive the non-logical aspects of our experience by means of an analytical dissociation whereby they are set apart. In this way we oppose them to the logical aspect of our thought and to each other in order to conceive them in a logical concept. But this analytical dissociation of the aspects presupposes their theoretical abstraction from the continuous bond of their coherence in the order of time. That is to say, we cannot get them in the grip of a logical concept without separating them from all the other aspects in an abstract logical discontinuity. But this does not mean a *real* elimination of their continuous bond of coherence, which, on the contrary, remains the necessary condition and presupposition of their theoretical dissociation and opposition. It merely proves the impossibility of conceiving the continuity of this coherence in an analytical way by theoretical thought.

Thus the first basic problem of our transcendental critique of theoretical thought may be more exactly formulated as follows: What is the continuous bond of coherence between the logical aspect and the non-logical aspects of our experience from which these aspects are abstracted in the theoretical attitude? And, how is the mutual relation between these aspects to be conceived?

By raising this problem we exclude in principle the false dogmatical idea that theoretical thought would be able to penetrate to empirical reality as it really is, or even to a metaphysical realm of being, which would be independent of possible human experience.

The false presupposition that the theoretical separation of the logical aspect from all the other aspects of our experience corresponds to true reality, has led to very singular metaphysical conclusions. The Greek philosopher, Aristotle, concluded from this presupposition that the theoretical-logical function of thought has an activity quite independent of the organic life of the body and the sense-organs. From this he derived his thesis that the active intellect is immortal in contrast to the individual man. He knew very well that the several concepts of theoretical thought are of an abstract character. But he did not realize that the separation of the logical function of thought itself from all the other aspects of our temporal experience is only a result of theoretical abstraction and can accordingly not agree with integral reality. The dogma concerning the autonomy of theoretical thought impeded the insight into its real structure.

This was also the reason why the fundamental difference between the theoretical and the non-theoretical attitude of thought was lost sight of, or was at least entirely misinterpreted. The non-theoretical attitude is that of the so-called naive experience, or of common sense experience. It lacks entirely that antithetical relation between the logical and the non-logical experiential modes, which is characteristic of the theoretical attitude of thought and experience. Here our logical function remains completely immerged in the continuity of the temporal coherence between the different aspects. Our attention is neither directed upon abstract special aspects of concrete phenomena, as in special scientific research, nor upon the inner nature and structure of the aspects as such, as in the philosophical theory concerning the fundamental modes of experience. Much rather we here experience concrete things and events in the typical structures of individual totalities which in principle function in all the modal aspects of our temporal horizon in their continuous mutual coherence. Our logical mode of distinction is entirely embedded in this integral experience. Our pre-theoretical logical concepts are only related to things and events as individual wholes, and not to the abstract modal aspects of their empirical reality. These aspects are only experienced implicitly in the things and events themselves, and not explicitly in their analytical dissociation and opposition to the logical function of thought.

It appears this can be refuted by examples.

Before we were able to abstract the numerical relations from concrete numerable things, we learned to count by means of an abacus or bead-frame by shifting the little red and white balls. All of us, in the naive attitude of experience, connect the spatial form of a circle to the representation of something round such as a hoop or wheel. All of us also connect the physico-chemical relations to concrete substances such as water, salt, and so forth; by no means do we have an abstract theoretical notion of energy relations as such. In the naive attitude of experience things are always conceived in the integral coherence of all their modal aspects.

How is this integral character of naive experience possible? How is it to be explained that even inanimate things and natural events such as a thunderstorm function in all the modal aspects of our naive experience in their continuous temporal bond of coherence? This is possible only by means of the subject-object relation which is inherent in this experiential attitude.

In this relation we ascribe to things and events objective functions in such aspects, in which they can never function as subjects.

As adults, who have outgrown infantile animistic representations, we know very well that water is not a living substance. Nevertheless, in the biotic aspect of our experience we ascribe to it the objective function of being a necessary means for life. We ascribe to it objective sensory qualities and some objective logical characteristics, objective functions in our socio-cultural life, and so forth. Notwithstanding the fact that in this subject-object relation water functions in all the modal aspects of our experience, we are aware of the fact that it belongs to the kingdom of inorganic matter, which is qualified by physico-chemical qualities.

A bird's nest, on the contrary, is typically qualified by its subject-object relation to the organic and sensory life of the bird, although we also ascribe to it objective functions in the post-biotic and post sensory aspects of our experiential horizon. In naive experience we conceive it as an individual whole, qualified by this subject-object relation to the bird's life; and this finds expression in the name whereby the thing is symbolically signified. The nest itself has an objective function in the aspect of symbolical signification. A plastic work of fine art is experienced as an individual whole, functioning in all the modal aspects of our temporal horizon, but typically qualified by its aesthetic subject-object relation. It expresses the aesthetic vision of the artist objectively in the material of his formation. A cathedral can only be experienced as an architectural whole, typically qualified by its objective destination, which finds expression in its entire inner structure, namely, that it has been destined for the use of the ecclesiastical cult. This means that its qualifying subject-object relation is only to be found in the modal aspect of faith, though it functions equally in all the other aspects of experience. We cannot, at this time, engage in a more detailed inquiry into the typical total structures of individuality, which the things display in naive experience.

In the present context we are interested only in the general significance of the subject-object relations which guarantee the integral character of this nontheoretic experience. By means of these relations the latter embraces in principle all the modal aspects of a thing or event in their continuous bond of coherence within the structural framework of an individual whole and without any analytical dissociation of these different aspects.

It is entirely foreign to naive experience to ascribe object functions to things or events apart from the possible subject functions to which they are related. The sensory color red is ascribed to a rose only in relation to every possible normal human sensory perception under adequate light conditions, not as an occult quality of a metaphysical substance which would exist in itself beyond any relation to possible sensory perception. This metaphysical conception is meaningless if the color red is understood as an objective sensory quality of the flower. If it is meant in the sense of the modern physical theory of light refraction, it is also meaningless since this theory does not relate to metaphysical substances, but to the energy-aspect of empirical phenomena.

The subject-object relations of naive experience are, consequently, fundamentally different from the antithetical relations which characterize the theoretical attitude of thought. Subject and object are certainly distinguished in the non-theoretical attitude, but they are never opposed to each other. Rather, they are conceived in an unbreakable coherence. In other words, naive experience leaves the integral structural coherence of our experiential horizon intact. The theoretical attitude of thought and experience breaks it asunder by an analytical dissociation of its modal aspects.

It is no wonder that modern philosophical theories of knowledge which hold to the dogma of the autonomy of theoretical thought, were incapable of doing justice to naive experience. Losing sight of the fundamental difference between the pre-theoretical subject-object relations inherent in naive experience and the antithetical relation characteristic of the theoretical attitude, they interpreted naive experience itself as an uncritical theory. This theory was called the theory of naive realism, or the copy-theory. According to this theory, naive experience was supposed to assume that our sensory perception gives us an adequate image of the things, as they are in themselves as metaphysical substances, apart from human experience. A refutation of this theory with the aid of the experimental results of scientific research on the one hand and epistemological arguments on the other, was supposed to be a refutation of naive experience itself. A strange misunderstanding, indeed!

Naive experience is not at all a theory which may be refuted by scientific and epistemological arguments. It does not identify empirical reality with its abstract sensory aspect and it lacks the metaphysical notion of an objective world of things in themselves beyond the world of experience. Naive experience is much rather a pre-theoretical datum, corresponding with the integral structure of our experiential horizon in its temporal order. Any philosophical theory of human experience which cannot account for this datum in a satisfactory way, must be erroneous in its fundamentals.

After this confrontation of the theoretical and the pretheoretical attitudes of thought and experience, we may continue our critical inquiry into the former. We have seen that the theoretical opposition of the logical function of thought to all the non-logical aspects of experience gives rise to the theoretical problem: How can we acquire a logical concept of these non-logical experiential modes? But theoretical philosophical thought cannot stop at this theoretical problem. It must proceed from the theoretical antithesis to a theoretical synthesis, or union, between the logical and the non-logical aspects if a logical concept of the non-logical modes of experience is to be possible.

When we reflect on this requirement, we are con-

fronted with a new fundamental problem which may
be formulated as follows: What is the central reference-point in our consciousness from which this theoretical synthesis can start?

Problem ② .

This question touches the core of our inquiry. By
raising this second basic problem, we subject every
possible starting-point of theoretical thought to our
transcendental criticism.

Now it is evident that the *true* starting-point of a
theoretical synthesis, or union, between the logical
and the non-logical experiential modes, howsoever it
may be chosen, is by no means to be found in one of
the terms of the antithetical relation. It must necessarily transcend the theoretical antithesis and relate
the aspects that were dissociated and opposed to one
another to a central unity in our consciousness. For
one thing is certain: the antithetical relation with
which the theoretical attitude of thought stands or
falls, offers in itself no bridge between the logical
aspect and the non-logical experiential modes opposed to it. And in the temporal order which guarantees their unbreakable coherence we do not find a
central reference-point, transcending the diversity of
the modal aspects.

This means that the dogma concerning the autonomy of theoretical thought must lead its adherents
into a seemingly inescapable *impasse*. To maintain
this autonomy, they are obliged to seek their starting-
point in theoretical thought itself. But by virtue of its
antithetic structure, this thought is bound to the in-
ter-modal theoretical synthesis between the logical

and the non-logical aspects. Even a so-called formal logic cannot do without a synthesis between the logical aspect and that of symbolical signification, which are by no means identical.

Now there are as many modalities of theoretical synthesis as there are experiential modes of a non-logical character. There is a synthetical thought of mathematical, physico-chemical, biological, psychological, historical, linguistic and others of like character. In which of these possible special theoretical viewpoints may philosophical thought find the starting-point of its theoretical and synthetical total view of our experiential horizon? No matter how the choice is made, it invariably amounts to the absolutizing of a synthetically conceived special modal aspect.

This is the source of all *isms* in the theoretical view of human experience and empirical reality. They result in the attempt to reduce all other modal aspects of our temporal horizon of experience to simple modalities of the absolutized aspect.

Now, such isms as mathematicism, biologism, sensualism, historicism, and so forth, are uncritical in a double respect. First, they are never to be justified from a purely theoretical standpoint. On the contrary, theoretical thought, because of its antithetical and synthetical character, is bound to the irreducible diversity of the fundamental modes of experience and their interrelations. In the whole sphere of theoretical thought there is nowhere room for the absoluteness of an aspect. The absolutization as such can, therefore, not originate in theoretical thought itself. It testifies much rather to the influence of supra-theo-retical motives which are masked by the pretended autonomy of philosophical thought.

Secondly, in every absolutization of a special syn-thetical viewpoint the fundamental problem concern-ing the starting-point of the theoretical synthesis returns unsolved. For this synthesis cannot nullify the irreducible diversity between the logical aspect and the non-logical experiential mode, which in the theo-retical antithesis, is made into its theoretical problem. Any attempt at reducing the logical term of the theoretical antithesis to the non-logical, or vice versa, is tantamount to a dogmatic elimination of the problem.

But is the above argument sufficient to demon-strate that philosophical thought, by virtue of its inner structure, cannot find its starting-point in itself? We should not draw this conclusion too hastily. Kant, the father of the so-called critical transcendental philoso-phy, was of the opinion that he could show a starting-point in theoretical thought itself, which is the central reference point of every special scientific synthesis and the condition of its possibility. Can the autonomy of theoretical thought be demonstrated by way of Kant's so-called critical transcendental method? Let us con-sider his argument.

To discover the immanent starting-point of theo-retical thought as the central reference-point of every theoretical synthesis, Kant points to the necessity of a critical self-reflection in our theoretical acts of think-ing by directing our reflection toward the thinking I.

crucial question !

This hint contains, indeed, a great promise. For it is beyond doubt that as long as theoretical thought in its logical function continues to be directed merely to the opposed modal aspects of our experiential horizon, it remains dispersed in the theoretical diversity of these aspects. Only when theoretical thought is directed toward the thinking *ego,* can it acquire the concentric direction towards an ultimate unity of our consciousness to which the whole modal diversity of our experiential horizon must be related. If you ask all the special sciences engaged in anthropological research: "What is man?" you will receive a great diversity of information referring to the different aspects of temporal human existence. These answers are, doubtless, important. But even by combining all these different special viewpoints from which they are given you cannot find an answer to the central question: "Who is man himself in the central unity of his selfhood?" The path of critical self-reflection is, consequently, the only one that can lead to the discovery of the true starting-point of philosophical thought.

But here a new fundamental problem arises, which may be formulated as follows: "How is the concentric direction of theoretical thought towards the ego possible, and what is its source?" It is beyond doubt that this problem, too, is of a truly transcendental nature. For by virtue of its dissociative character theoretical thought is bound to an antithetic basic relation, which as such can only lead it in a divergent direction.

Consequently, the concentric direction of theoretical thought upon the human selfhood cannot orig-

inate from theoretical reason itself. Nevertheless, self- *why not?*
reflection is necessary in a transcendental critique to
reveal the real starting-point of philosophical thinking. Kant did not raise the problem mentioned since
he held to the dogma of the autonomy of theoretical
thought. Therefore he was obliged to seek the central
reference-point of the theoretical synthesis in the
logical aspect of thought, which he calls understanding.

The notion, "I think," so he says, must necessarily
accompany all my representations if they are to be
altogether my representations. But this "I think" is
according to him only that subjective logical pole of
thought which can never become the object of my
thinking since it is the logical center from which every
act of thinking must start.

Kant calls this supposed logical center of theoretical
thought the "transcendental logical unity of apper-
ception," or also the transcendental logical subject,
or "ego." He assumes that it is a subjective logical
unity of an absolutely simple character, so that it is
indeed a central unity without a single multiplicity
or diversity of components. This transcendental-
logical *I* is, according to Kant, to be distinguished
sharply from the empirical ego, the psycho-physical
human person, which we can perceive in time and
space. It does not belong to empirical reality. It is
much rather the general condition of any possible act
of thought; and as such it has no individuality of any
kind. It is the theoretical-logical subject to which all

empirical reality can be opposed as its objective counter-pole, its object of knowledge and experience.

Kant emphasizes that from this transcendental logical notion, "I think," not an iota of self-knowledge is to be gained, since our knowledge is restricted to the sensorily perceptible phenomena in time and space, which are the very object of the logical I. But has Kant succeeded in showing a real starting-point of the theoretical synthesis within the logical aspect of thought itself? The answer must be negative. We have seen that the reference-point of the theoretical synthesis cannot be found within the theoretical anti-thesis between the logical aspect and the non-logical aspects of experience, which are made into the prob-lem of analytical inquiry. But Kant's transcendental logical subject is exactly conceived of as the subjec-tive-logical pole of this antithesis. As such it can never be the central reference-point of our experience in the temporal order with its diversity of modal aspects.

The "cogito" from which Kant starts cannot be a merely logical unity. It implies the fundamental rela-tion between the ego and its acts of thought, which can by no means be identical. A logical unity, on the other hand, can never be an absolute unity without multiplicity. This contradicts the modal nature of the logical aspect. Thus Kant's view of the transcendental ego lands in pure mythology. It implies an intrin-sically contradictory identification of the central I with its subjective logical function.

To maintain the dogma of the autonomy of theo-retical thought Kant has allowed the real starting-point of his critique of theoretical reason to remain in the dark. It is the task of our radical critique to uncover it.

The third transcendental problem, which we have raised, namely, "How is the concentric direction of theoretical thought upon the ego possible, and whence does it originate?" cannot be solved without knowing the inner nature of the human *I*, i. e., without self-knowledge. Since the days of Socrates, philosophy has sought for this self-knowledge. But the human I as the center of human experience and existence, displays an enigmatic character.

As soon as I try to grasp the I in a philosophical concept it recedes as a phantom and dissolves itself into nothingness. It cannot be determined by any modal aspect of our experience, since it is the central reference-point to which all fundamental modes of our temporal experience are related. A logical I does not exist, neither a psycho-physical I, nor a historical, nor a moral I. All such philosophical determinations of the ego disregard its central character.

David Hume was quite right when, from his sensualistic viewpoint, he dissolved the concept of the selfhood into a natural relation between our successive sensations. The Socratic requirement: "Know yourself," leads philosophical reflection to the limits of all theoretical thought. Must the philosopher stop at these limits in order to save the dogma of the autonomy of theoretical reason? But this would be pure self-deceit, since without a radical critical self-reflection we ignore the inescapable transcendental problems implied in the intrinsical nature of the theoretical attitude of philosophical thought itself. The uncritical absolutization to which the ignoring of these problems has led makes it necessary to overcome also this last bulwark of theoretical dogmatism. This can be done by directing our theoretical thought to its central supra-theoretical reference-point, the human I, or selfhood.

It is not theoretical thought that can give itself this concentric direction. It is the central ego which alone can do so, from a supra-theoretical starting-point. What is the inner nature of this enigmatical I? And how can we arrive at real self-knowledge? These central questions will be the subject-matter of our second lecture on the general subject of the pretended autonomy of reason.

The Pretended Autonomy
of Philosophical Thought—II

The consideration of the concentric direction of our theoretical thought upon the human ego appeared to be necessary in order to discover the real starting-point of philosophical reflection. This consideration, however, gave rise to a new problem, which we formulated as follows: How is this concentric direction possible and what is its real origin? This problem has not as yet found a solution, but it fixed our attention upon the enigmatical character of this I. The latter turned out to be the central reference-point of our entire temporal horizon of experience with its diversity of modal aspects. As such it turned out to be also the real center of every theoretical act of thinking, and, consequently, a necessary presupposition of philosophical thought in all of its manifestations.

But each attempt to grasp this central ego in a logical concept and to define it with the aid of synthetically conceived modal aspects of our temporal experiential horizon appeared to be doomed to failure.

The mystery of the central human ego is that it is

nothing in itself, i. e., viewed apart from the central
relations wherein alone it presents itself. But the first
of these relations, namely, that of the selfhood to the
temporal horizon of our experience cannot determine
the inner character of the ego, except in a negative
sense. The central unity of the selfhood is not to be
found in the modal diversity of the temporal order.
A physico-psychical I does not exist, neither a logical,
a historical, nor a moral self.

However, let us turn to the other central relations
wherein our ego functions, in order to consider
whether they can determine the inner nature of our
ego in a positive sense. Contemporary personalistic
and existentialistic philosophy have laid all the
stress upon the interpersonal I-thou relation, which
is essential to self-knowledge. The Jewish thinker,
Martin Buber, sharply contrasts this inter-personal
relation to the subject-object relation of our experience. In his opinion, the former reveals itself in a
real spiritual meeting of the persons concerned, the
latter, in contrast, gives expression only to a ruler's
attitude, inherent in experience, which objectifies the
world in order to control it. Disregarding Buber's
view of experience, which apparently is oriented to
the Humanist science ideal in its natural scientific
sense, we must posit that, in any case, experience and
the inter-personal relation cannot be contrasted to one
another. Experience itself implies an inter-personal relationship between one ego and another. This
relation belongs to the central sphere of our experiential horizon and eliminating it amounts to anni-

hilating self-consciousness. My selfhood is nothing without that of yours, and that of our fellow-men. In other words there exists a central communal relation between the individual centers of experience, lying at the foundation also of any temporal communal relation in theoretical thought.

But can this central I-thou relation give a positive content to our self-consciousness? Can it lead us to a solution of the riddle of the human ego? So long as it is viewed only in itself, this relation is no more able to do so than the relation of our ego to the temporal horizon of our experience. The reason is that the ego of our fellow-men confronts us with the same mystery as our own selfhood. The Swiss psychiatrist and philosopher, Binswanger, strongly influenced by contemporary existentialism and personalism, says that the communal relation of you-I is qualified as an inter-personal meeting in *love*. But what is meant by this meeting in love? Within the temporal horizon of our experience the love-relation displays a great diversity of modal meaning and typical societal structures. There is a difference in principle between the sexual eros, or affection, as an instinctive sexual drive, and the moral love of the neighbor. Both, in turn, differ in principle from the theoretical Platonic love of beauty, truth and goodness. The love between husband and wife, or that between parents and their children is of a different typical societal character from the love between a venerated master and his disciples, or from our inter-personal relations to our compatriots, implied in the common love of country.

But none of these temporal love-relations can be of that central nature which is essential to the human selfhood.

It may be that there exists a central love-relation which is capable of determining the inner meaning of my ego in its essential communal relation to that of my fellowmen. But as long as this love-relation is only viewed as a temporal relation between me and my fellowmen, we must posit that we do not know what is really meant by it. And as long as terms such as *interpersonal meeting* and *love* are used in philosophical anthropology in an undefined sense, a suspicion of mystification is bound to arise.

Both the central relations, which we have considered up to this point, are empty in themselves, just like the human ego that functions in them.

But there is a third central relation which points above the human selfhood to its divine Origin. This is the central religious relation between the human ego and God, in whose image man was created. It may be objected that this relation exceeds the boundaries of philosophical thought. This is certainly true, since philosophical thought is bound to the temporal horizon of experience with its modal diversity of aspects.

Nevertheless, it can only be this religious relation from which philosophical thought in its theoretical attitude can acquire the concentric direction upon our selfhood. For it is beyond doubt, that theoretical thought, viewed apart from the central ego, cannot give itself this central direction. It is only the thinking I that is capable of critical self-reflection.

But if our philosophical thought is not directed upon that central religious relation, which points above the thinking ego to its absolute Origin, all critical self-reflection is doomed to result in the conclusion that the ego is nothing. This conclusion, however, is meaningless, since it would imply the negation of theoretical thought itself; for the latter is nothing without the ego. Thus a philosophical self-reflection which is not directed upon the central religious relation will be obliged to seek the ego within the temporal horizon of our experience in order to avoid this nihilistic result. Thereby it abandons the critical attitude and devises an idol of the central ego by absolutizing one of the modal aspects of our temporal consciousness. This is the origin of such idols as the psychological, the transcendental-logical, the historical and the moral ego.

However, we have established that such absolutizations are not to be explained on the basis of theoretical thought itself. They rather betray the influence of a supra-theoretical central motive, which can only be of a religious character. For it is only in its central religious relation to its divine origin that the thinking ego can direct itself and the modal diversity of its temporal world upon the absolute. The inner tendency to do so is an innate religious impulsion of the ego. For, as the concentration point of all meaning, which it finds dispersed in the modal diversity of its temporal horizon of experience, the human ego points above itself to the Origin of all meaning, whose absoluteness reflects itself in the human ego as the central seat of the image of God. This ego, which is empty in itself, is only determined in a positive sense by its concentric relation to its divine origin. And it is also from this central relation that the relation of our ego to its temporal horizon and its central communal relation to the ego of our fellow-man can take a positive content.

The innate religious impulsion of the ego in which its central relation to its divine Origin finds expression, takes its content from a religious basic motive as the central spiritual motive power of our thinking and acting. If this basic motive is of an apostate character it will turn the ego away from its true Origin and direct its religious impulse upon our temporal horizon of experience, to seek within the latter both itself and its Origin. This will give rise to idols originating from the absolutization of what has only a relative meaning. But even in this apostate manifestation the religious character of the selfhood, as the point of concentration of human nature, continues to reveal itself. Even in its absolutizing of the relative, the thinking and acting ego transcends its temporal horizon. It is subjected to a central law that we may call the religious concentration law of our consciousness, by which it is obliged to transcend itself in order to find the positive meaning of itself.

Therefore, the real starting-point of philosophical thought cannot be the ego in itself, which is an empty notion. It can only be the religious basic motive, operative in the ego as the center of our temporal horizon of experience. This alone gives the ego its positive dynamic character also in its central interpersonal relation to the other egos and to its temporal world. In other words, such a basic motive implies the three central relations in which the ego can only manifest itself.

As soon as philosophical thought begins to lose its definite direction in consequence of the undermining of its religious basic motive, it falls into a state of spiritual decadence and becomes a victim to a radical relativism and nihilism. At present the symptoms of such a spiritual uprooting can readily be established in what is called the fundamental crisis of contemporary, secularized Western thought. In this crisis the distress and disintegration of the human ego itself is revealed. For the ego necessarily dissolves itself into nothingness when it loses its direction towards the Absolute which even in its idolatry it seeks to preserve.

The religious basic motive is always of a central communal character and gives expression to a common spirit which unites those who are ruled by it. It rules a thinker even when, in consequence of the traditional dogma concerning the autonomy of philosophical thought, he is not aware of its true nature. As a communal motive it lies at the foundation of a community of thought, insofar as it guarantees an ultimate possibility of mutual understanding even between philosophical trends which vehemently combat one another.

Within the temporal order of our experiential horizon, to which our philosophical thought is bound, the influence of the religious basic motive upon philosophy is bound to two conditions. First, it must give rise to a common belief within the faith-aspect of our experience; secondly, it must gain a socio-cultural power within the historical aspect of human society, so that it has become a formative factor in human culture. The faith-power, which it develops in its temporal manifestation, makes it into the leading principle of our thought. The socio-cultural power, which it has acquired in the process of history, guarantees the temporal foundation of its social influences. The faith-aspect of its manifestation within the temporal horizon of experience can be made into the theoretical object of a theological investigation. The historico-cultural aspect of its influence can be made into the theoretical object of historical research. But the religious basic motive itself in its central sense can no more become the object of a theoretical inquiry than the central ego itself.

In our transcendental critique, this religious basic motive is only to be approached in the concentric direction of our theoretical thought on the thinking ego. But this thinking ego is then to be taken in its positive sense as the religious center of our temporal experience, which, as such, transcends the bounds of philosophical thought, but is nevertheless its necessary presupposition.

If the religious basic motives did not manifest their central influence within the inner development of philosophical thought itself, philosophy would have nothing to do with them. But it is the very task of a radical transcendental critique to show this influence in order to break through any form of theoretical dogmatism which masks its true starting-point by the deceptive axiom of the autonomy of theoretical reason.

And our previous inquiry into the inner structure of the theoretical attitude of thought, and the formulation of the three transcendental basic problems to which this attitude gives rise, have uncovered the necessary inner point of connection between the theoretical sphere of our philosophical reflection and the central supra-theoretical sphere of our consciousness, which is of a religious character.

The development of Western philosophy has been chiefly ruled by four religious basic motives, which have acquired a socio-cultural power in the history of Western civilization. The first is the Greek form-matter motive, whose religious meaning I shall explain presently. The second is the radical biblical basic motive of creation, fall into sin, and redemption by Jesus Christ in the communion of the Holy Spirit; the third is the scholastic motive of nature and grace; the fourth is the modern Humanistic motive of nature and freedom.

Before engaging in a brief explanation of these four basic motives, and of their central influence upon philosophical thought, I will make some remarks concerning the general character of the non-biblical ones.

In contrast to the central motive of the Holy Scriptures, they present a dialectical character. This means that they are intrinsically divided by an irrevocable religious antithesis, caused by the fact that they are composed of two central motive powers, which are polarly in opposition to one another. They involve every philosophical thought that finds itself in their grip, in a dialectial process, wherein this thought is alternately driven towards the one or the other pole of its religious starting-point. What is the origin of this intrinsic conflict in the dialectical basic motives? As to the scholastic motive of nature and grace, it originates from the attempt at a mutual accommodation of the biblical and the Greek or Humanistic basic motives, which exclude one another in principle. As to the Greek and the Humanistic motives, their inner conflict originates in the fact that they divert the innate religious impulse of the human ego from its true Origin and direct it upon the temporal horizon of experience with its diversity of modal aspects. By seeking itself and its absolute origin in one of these aspects, the thinking I turns to the absolutization of the relative.

Now I have shown in the preceding lecture on this same subject that the modal sense of every experiential aspect can only reveal itself in an unbreakable correlation with that of all the others. This means that the religious absolutization of particular aspects cannot fail to call forth their correlates, which in the religious consciousness begin to claim an absoluteness opposite to that of the deified ones.

In other words, any idol that has been created by the absolutization of a modal aspect evokes its counter idol.

Consequently, the dialectical basic motives are always characterized by an ultimate antithesis. This antithesis divides the religious impulse of the ego and thereby prevents the insight into the radical unity of the human selfhood in its central relation to the whole of our temporal horizon of experience.

It is impossible to solve this antithesis by means of a genuine synthesis. The reason is that this antithesis urges itself upon the human consciousness with the mythical semblance of being absolute and it does so with an inner necessity because of its religious character.

This is the fundamental difference between a theoretical and a religious dialectic. The former is inherent in the antithetical relation which characterizes the theoretical attitude of thought. It requires a theoretical synthesis between the logical aspect of our thought and the non-logical experiential aspects which we have set in opposition to it and which constitute its field of research. And this synthesis turned out to require a starting-point in the central religious sphere of our consciousness. But when this central starting-point itself presents an antithesis between two opposed motive powers, there is no other central starting-point to be found to solve this antithesis by means of an ultimate synthesis. The religious antithesis does not allow any real solution so long as the human ego finds itself in the grip of the dialectical basic motive that has called it into being. In this case there remains no other way out than to attribute the primacy to one of the opposed motives, which implies a religious depreciation, or at least, a subordination of the other. The periodic shifting of the primacy from the one motive to the other causes a dialectical process in philosophical thought that has its central starting-point in such a dialectical basic motive. This is why one and the same dualistic basic motive can give rise to polarly opposed philosophical tendencies, which at first sight seem to have nothing in common.

It is a regular phenomenon in the development of the religious dialectic in its expression within a philosophical course of thought that after or before a critical phase leading to a sharp separation of the two opposite motives, there arises a tendency to reconcile them by means of a so-called dialectical logic. Such an attempt testifies to the lack of a critical mind in philosophical reflection.

or a mind that sees the alternative but will not accept it.

Therefore it is no wonder that the imaginary synthesis effected by means of such a dialectical logic dissolves itself again into a definite antithesis as soon as philosophy arrives at or returns to a critical attitude. We meet with all these traits of a dialectical process in the development of Western philosophy insofar as it has been ruled by the three dialectical basic motives mentioned.

and just how far is it so ruled?

This will appear in the second part of this lecture, in which we shall explain the influence of these motives upon Western thought.

*   *   *

The central motive of Greek philosophy, which we

have designated as the form-matter motive in line
with the Aristotelian terminology, originated from
the meeting of the pre-Homeric religion of life and
death, with the younger, cultural religion of the
Olympian gods. The older religion deified the ever-
flowing stream of organic life, which issues from
mother earth and cannot be bound to any individual
form. In consequence, the deities of this religion are
amorphous. It is from this shapeless stream of ever-
flowing organic life that the generations of perishable
beings originate periodically, whose existence, limited
by a corporeal form, is subjected to the horrible fate
of death, designated by the Greek terms *anangkē* or
heimarmenē tuchē. This existence in a limiting form
was considered an injustice since it is obliged to
sustain itself at the cost of other beings so that the
life of one is the death of another. Therefore all fixa-
tion of life in an individual figure is avenged by the
merciless fate of death in the order of time. This is
the meaning of the mysterious utterance of the ancient
Greek philosopher, Anaximander, which reads: "the
(divine) Origin of all things is the *apeiron*" (that is
to say, that which lacks a limiting form). "The things
return to that from which they originate according
to destiny. For they pay to each other penalty and
retribution of their injustice in the order of time."

The central motive of this religion, consequently,
is that of the shapeless stream of life eternally flowing
throughout the process of birth and decline of all that
exists in a corporeal form. This is the original religious sense of the matter-principle in Greek philosophy.

It issued from a deification of the biotic aspect of our temporal horizon of experience and has found its most suggestive expression in the ecstatic cult of Dionysus, imported from Thrace.

The form-motive, on the other hand, was the central motive of the younger Olympian religion, the religion of form, measure and harmony. It was rooted in the deification of the cultural aspect of classical Greek society. This motive found its most profound expression in the cult of the Delphian god, Apollo, the legislator. The Olympian gods have left mother earth with its ever-flowing stream of organic life and its inescapable *anangkē*. They have acquired the Olympus as their residence and have a personal and immortal form, imperceptible to the eye of sense, an ideal form of a perfect and splendid beauty, the genuine prototype of the Platonic idea as the imperishable metaphysical form of true being. But these immortal gods have no power over the *anangkē*, the inexorable fate of death. Remember the utterance of Homer in his Odyssey: "The immortals too cannot help lamentable man when the cruel *anangkē* strikes him down."

This is why the younger Olympian religion was only accepted as the public religion of the Greek polis, the city-State. But in their private life the Greeks continued to hold to the old earthly gods of life and death.

The form-matter motive, originating in the religious consciousness of the Greeks, from the meeting of these two antagonistic religions, was, as such not de-

pendent upon the mythological and ritual forms of
the latter. As its central basic motive it ruled Greek
thought from the very beginning. The autonomy
claimed by Greek philosophical theories over against
the popular belief, implied merely an abandonment
of the mythological forms of the latter which were
bound to sensuous representation. It did not mean a
break with the form-matter motive, as such, which
was much rather the common religious starting-point
of all Greek thinkers. It was this very basic motive,
which alone guaranteed a real community of thought
between Greek philosophical tendencies, polarly opposed to one another. It determined the Greek view
of nature, or *physis,* which excluded in principle the
biblical idea of creation; it also ruled the classical
Greek meaning of the terms *eidos* and *idea,* which is
only understandable from the religious significance
of the Greek form-motive. It lay at the foundation
both of the Greek metaphysical view of being in its
opposition to the visible world of becoming and decline, and of the Greek views of human nature and
human society. Because of its dialectical character, it
has involved Greek thought in a dialectical process
that displays all the traits which we have briefly
indicated.

* * *

The second basic motive of Western thought is the
radical and central biblical theme of creation, fall
into sin and redemption by Jesus Christ as the in-

carnate Word of God, in the communion of the Holy Spirit.

This basic motive is the central spiritual motive power of every Christian thought worthy of this name. It should not be confounded with the ecclesiastical articles of faith, which refer to this motive, and which can be made into the object of a dogmatic theological reflection in the theoretical attitude of thought. As the core of the divine Word-revelation, it is independent of any human theology. Its radical sense can only be explained by the Holy Spirit, operating in the heart, or the religious center of our consciousness, within the communion of the invisible Catholic church.

This basic religious motive has uncovered the real root, or center, of human nature and unmasks the idols of the human ego, which arise by seeking this center within the temporal horizon of our experience with its modal diversity of aspects. It reveals the real positive meaning of the human ego, as the religious concentration-point of our integral existence, as the central seat of the *imago Dei* in the positive direction of the religious impulse of the ego upon its absolute Origin. Furthermore, it uncovers the origin of all absolutizations of the relative, namely, the negative, or apostate direction of the religious impulse of the human ego. Thereby it reveals the real character of all basic motives of human thought, which divert the religious impulse towards the temporal horizon. This, then, is also the radical critical significance of the biblical basic motive for philosophy, since it frees the

[margin note: v. important statement of Frame's paper.]

thinking ego from the prejudices, which, in principle, because of their originating from absolutizations impede a philosophical insight into the real and integral structure of the temporal order of experience.

As such this biblical basic motive is the only possible starting-point of a Christian philosophy in its genuine sense. But the development of such a philosophy has been prevented again and again by the powerful influence of Greek philosophy, and later on by the rise of the scholastic basic motive of nature and grace.

In the first phase of Christian thought, in which the Augustinian influence was predominant, the central working of this biblical basic motive was restricted to dogmatical theology. The latter was erroneously identified with Christian philosophy, which implied that philosophical questions were only treated within a theological context. Accordingly, the Augustinian rejection of the autonomy of philosophical thought over against the divine Word-revelation amounted to the denial of this autonomy over against dogmatical theology, which was considered the queen of the sciences. This latter view was not biblical at all, but rather taken from the Aristotelian metaphysics, which had ascribed this royal position to a philosophical theology of which all other sciences would be the slaves. In fact, the philosophical fundamentals of Augustine's thought were, in the main, taken from the Hellenistic philosophy and only externally accommodated to the doctrine of the Church.

In the second phase, beginning with the rise of

Thomism, philosophy and dogmatical theology were sharply distinguished. But at the same time a third religious basic motive arose, which excluded the radical and integral influence of the central biblical motive on philosophy. This is the motive of *nature and grace*, which ever since has been the starting-point of scholastic philosophy as it developed both in Roman Catholic and Protestant circles. It originally aimed at a mutual accommodation of the biblical and the Greek religious basic motives. But since the Renaissance it could also be serviceable to a mutual accommodation of the biblical and the modern Humanistic starting-points. It implied the distinction between a natural and a supra-natural sphere of thought and acting.

Within the natural sphere a relative autonomy was ascribed to human reason, which was supposed to be capable of discovering the natural truths by its own light. Within the supra-natural sphere of grace, on the contrary, human thought was considered to be dependent on the divine self-revelation. Philosophy was considered to belong to the natural sphere, dogmatical theology, on the other hand, to the supra-natural sphere. In consequence, there was no longer a question of Christian philosophy. Philosophical thought was, in fact, abandoned to the influence of the Greek and Humanist basic motives in their external accommodation to the doctrine of the Church. These motives were masked by the dogmatic acceptance of the autonomy of natural reason. The scholastic meaning ascribed to this autonomy was determined by the nature-grace-theme. Natural reason should not contradict the supra-natural truths of the Church's doctrine, based on divine revelation. This implied an external accommodation of either the Greek or the Humanistic philosophical conceptions to this ecclesiastical doctrine as long as the ecclesiastical authority was factually respected by the students of philosophy. The Thomistic attempt at a synthesis of the opposite motives of nature and grace, and the ascription of the primacy to the latter found a clear expression in the adage: *Gratia naturam non tollit, sed perficit* (Grace does not cancel nature, but it perfects it).

But the dialectical character of the nature-grace motive clearly manifested itself in the late medieval nominalistic movement. The Thomistic synthesis of nature and grace was replaced by a sharp antithesis. Any point of connection between the natural and the supernatural sphere was denied. This was the introduction to the shifting of primacy to the nature-motive. The process of secularization of philosophy had started.

The fourth religious basic motive which has acquired a central influence on Western thought is that of modern Humanism, which has arisen since the Italian Renaissance of the 15th century. Since Immanuel Kant this has in general been designated as the theme of *nature* and *freedom*. Under the influence of the dogma of the autonomy of philosophical thought, its religious sense was camouflaged. Consequently, it was presented as a purely philosophical theme concerning the relation between theoretical and practical reason, a theme equally discussed in Greek and scholastic philosophy. In the same way, the Greek form-matter motive was presented in scholastic philosophy as a purely philosophical axiom concerning a primordial metaphysical distinction implied in the fundamental idea of being. A radical transcendental critique of philosophical thought should not be led astray by such axiomatic assertions. In fact, the Humanistic freedom-motive and its dialectical counterpart, the Humanist nature-motive, were of a central religious character. The freedom-motive originates in a religion of humanity, into which the biblical basic-motive had been completely transformed. The *renascimento* device of the Italian Renaissance meant a real rebirth of man into a new, creative and entirely new, personality. This personality was thought of as absolute in itself and was considered to be the only ruler of its own destiny and that of the world. This meant a Copernican revolution with respect to the biblical basic-motive of the Christian religion. The biblical revelation of the creation of man in the image of God was implicitly subverted into the idea of a creation of God in the idealized image of man. The biblical conception of the rebirth of man and his radical freedom in Jesus Christ was replaced by the idea of a regeneration of man by his own autonomous will, his emancipation from the medieval kingdom of darkness, rooted in the belief of the supra-natural authority of the Church.

This new Humanistic freedom-motive, which was foreign to Greek thought since it presupposed the

Christian motive of creation, fall into sin and redemption, called forth a new view of nature, which was conceived as the macro-cosmic counterpart of the new, religious personality-ideal. The so-called discovery of nature, in the Renaissance, had an indubitable religious background. After having emancipated himself from all belief in a supra-natural sphere in its scholastic-ecclesiastical sense, and having made himself into the only master of his destiny, modern man seeks in nature infinite possibilities to satisfy his own creative impulse. He considers the macrocosm from the optimistic viewpoint of his own expectation of the future. This means that the scholastic conception of the divine creator as *natura naturans* is transferred to the new image of nature. The adage, *Deus sive natura,* current in the Italian Renaissance testifies to a deification of the new image of nature, which is radically different from the deification of the ever-flowing stream of life in the old Ionian philosophy of nature.

The revolution brought about later on by Copernicus in the astronomic image of the universe, was considered by the rising Humanism, as a consequence of the religious revolution caused by the rebirth (*renascimento*) device of the Italian Renaissance. The modern autonomous man recreates both his divine Origin and his world in his own image.

But the new freedom-motive, just like its correlative, the new nature-motive, includes a diversity of possible tendencies. The reason is that it lacks the radical unity of sense proper to the biblical conception of Christian freedom, which concerns the true root and center of human existence. Much rather, it again diverts the concentric religious impulse of the human ego towards the temporal horizon of our experience with its diversity of modal aspects. This means that the Humanist basic-motive does not imply a univocal answer to the question: Where is the central seat of man's autonomous liberty to be found? Neither does it furnish a univocal answer to the question: What is the relation between man's free and autonomous personality and the realm of nature, and, under which viewpoint can nature be conceived as a unity? From the Humanist starting-point the center of man's autonomous and creative freedom might be sought in the moral, or in the aesthetic, in the theoretic-logical or in the sensitive aspect of our temporal experiential horizon. In the same way the unity of nature as the macro-cosmic universe could be conceived under different absolutized modal viewpoints.

Nevertheless, there was from the very beginning a strong tendency in the freedom-motive to strive after the rulership over nature, and this tendency, too, testifies to the influence of the secularized biblical creation-motive on the Humanist starting-point. For the biblical revelation concerning the creation of man in the image of God is immediately followed by the great cultural commandment that man should subject the earth and have the rule over it. As soon as the tendency to dominate the temporal world acquired the upperhand, in the Humanist freedom-motive,

the central seat of man's autonomous freedom is
sought in mathematical thought. In sharp contrast
with the Greek and medieval conception of mathe-
matics, a creative power was ascribed to mathematical
analysis, viewed as the universal foundation of logic.
The Humanist freedom-motive does not allow the
acceptance of a given structural order of creation
within the temporal horizon of experience. This
would contradict the Humanist meaning of the
autonomy of theoretical thought, which is fundamentally different both from the Greek and from the
scholastic view of this autonomy. Therefore the
Cartesian renovation of the methodical fundamentals
of philosophy implied a theoretical destruction of the
entire given structural order of human experience,
in order to reconstruct the material world *more
geometrico.*

The impulse to dominate nature by an autonomous
scientific thought required a deterministic image of
the world, construed as an uninterrupted chain of
functional causal relations, to be formulated in
mathematical equations. Galileo and Newton laid the
foundations of classical mathematical physics. To construct an image of the world corresponding with the
domination-motive, the method of this special science
was elevated to a universal pattern of scientific philosophic thought. Nature was conceived as a central
unity under the absolutized mechanistic viewpoint.
But now the inner religious dialectic of the Humanistic basic motive began to reveal itself in modern
philosophy. The mechanistic world-image constructed

under the primacy of the nature-motive, aiming at the sovereign domination of the world, left no room for the autonomous freedom of human personality in its practical activity. Nature and freedom appeared to be opposite motives in the Humanistic starting-point.

Henceforth Humanist philosophy was involved in a restless dialectical process. With Rousseau, the primacy is transferred to the freedom-motive and the central seat of human freedom is sought in the modal aspect of feeling. Kant's critical philosophy led to a sharp separation of the realms of nature and freedom. The nature motive was depreciated. The mathematical and mechanistic science-ideal was restricted to an empirical world of sensory phenomena ordered by transcendental logical categories of the human understanding. The autonomous freedom of man does not belong to the sensory realm of nature but to the supra-sensory realm of ethics, which is not ruled by natural laws, but by norms. As in Rousseau, the religious primacy was ascribed to the freedom-motive. But the central seat of human freedom was now sought in the moral aspect of the human will.

Post-Kantian idealism seeks to overcome Kant's critical dualism by a dialectical mode of thought which was supposed to bring about an ultimate synthesis of nature and freedom.

The mathematical science-ideal, born from the impulse to dominate nature, is replaced by another philosophical pattern of thought, oriented to the historical aspect of experience. This gives rise to a his-

toricistic view of the temporal world, which reduces
all the other aspects of our experience to the historical
one. The new historical mode of thought is polarly
opposed to the rationalistic and individualistic
method of thinking, which originated from the mathematical and mechanistic science-ideal. It is inspired
by an irrationalistic and universalistic turn in the Humanist freedom-motive. But in the middle of the last
century the German freedom-idealism broke down,
and gave place to a naturalistic positivism. The
nature-motive regained the upperhand and the historical mode of thought was transformed into a more
complicated kind of natural scientific thinking. Meanwhile, historicism, no longer checked by the belief in
eternal ideas of the human reason, began to display its
relativistic consequences, resulting in a process of
spiritual uprooting of Western thought. The former
Humanistic belief itself was viewed as a mere historical phenomenon, the perishable product of our
Western cultural mind. The transitory influence of
neo-Kantianism and neo-Hegelianism could not stop
this process. Both contemporary logical positivism and
its polar opposite, Humanistic existentialism, testify
to a fundamental crisis of Humanist philosophy.

* * *

This brief survey of the central significance of the
religious basic-motives of Western thought may suffice
to show the necessity of a radical transcendental
critique of philosophical thinking.

The central influence of the religious motives upon philosophical thought is mediated by a threefold transcendental basic idea that, consciously or unconsciously, is laid to the foundation of any philosophical reflection and which alone makes such reflection possible. This threefold basic idea, which I have called the "cosmonomic idea" of philosophy, is related to the three primordial transcendental basic problems concerning the theoretical attitude of thought, as such, which we have formulated and considered in our first lecture. Consequently, it contains first a transcendental limiting idea of the whole of our temporal horizon of experience with its modal diversity of aspects, including a view of the mutual relation between these aspects; secondly, an idea of the central reference-point of all synthetical acts of thought; and, in the third place, an idea of the Origin, whether or not it is called God, relating all that is relative to the absolute.

Though such a transcendental basic idea is a general and necessary condition of philosophical thought, the positive content given to it is dependent upon the central basic motive which rules the thinking ego. This implies that even the transcendental critique of philosophy which I have briefly explained in these two lectures could not be independent of my own religious starting-point. This gives rise to two critical questions which you will doubtless ask me at the conclusion of my explanation. First: How can this criticism have any conclusive force for those who do not accept your religious starting-point? And, second:

What may be the common basis for a philosophical ② discussion between those who lack a common starting-point?

As to the first question, I may reply that my criticism of theoretical thought had no other aim primarily, than to lay bare the structural data of our temporal horizon of experience and of the theoretical attitude of thinking, both of which are of general validity. But I have also shown why these structural data were inevitably lost from sight as long as the dogma concerning the autonomy of theoretical reason impeded a radical transcendental critique of philosophical thought. Under the influence of unrecognized absolutizations of theoretical abstractions there arose a diversity of opposing philosophical views concerning human experience and empirical reality, lacking a truly critical verification. And the absolutizations, as it turned out, originated from dialectical basic-motives of a religious character. The radical biblical basic motive unmasks any absolutization of the relative, and may free philosophical thought from dogmatic prejudices, which impede an integral view of the real structures of human experience. This effect is verifiable since it manifests itself within the temporal experiential horizon, whose structural order has a general validity for every thinker.

This certainly does not mean that our transcendental critique, since it starts from this radical basic motive, may lay claim to a philosophical infallibility. This supposition would testify to a philosophical self-exaltation, which originates in the lack of true self-knowledge. Every philosophical reflection is a fallible human activity and a Christian philosophy has, as such, no privileged position in this respect. It is only its biblical basic-motive that can give it a truly Christian character and free it from dogmatic prejudices, which impede insight into the integral order of human experience founded in divine creation.

Structural data, founded in the temporal order of human experience, however, are facts of a transcendental significance, which should be acknowledged, irrespective of their philosophical interpretation. If these data seem not to agree with certain dogmatical presuppositions of a philosophical school, the adherents of the latter should not try to eliminate the data, but to find a satisfactory philosophical explanation upon the basis of their own starting-point. Every philosophical current may contribute to the testing of its own and other philosophical views with respect to data, which up to now have been neglected. For the discovery of this neglected state of affairs in our experiential horizon is not the monopoly of a particular philosophical school. Thanks to common grace, relative truths are to be found in every philosophy, although the interpretation of such truths may appear to be unacceptable from the biblical standpoint insofar as the philosophical interpretation turns out to be ruled by a dialectical and apostate basic motive. However, no philosophy can prosper in isolation.

Here I arrive at the second question: What may be the common basis for a philosophical discussion between those who do not share a common starting-point? I think the first condition for finding such a common basis should be the conviction that any serious philosophical current has to contribute in its own way to the fulfillment of the common philosophical task of mankind. This conviction should be at the foundation of every philosophical debate even though the views concerning the task of philosophy may diverge to a high degree, and, although the philosophical basic ideas are ruled by unbiblical motives and hence, fundamentally erroneous. Therefore, the barren exclusivistic attitude of the schools, in which each of them, according to its adherents, was supposed to have the monoply of philosophical truth, should be broken down.

The chief cause of this exclusivism was the dogmatic absolutization of specific patterns of thought and the lack of insight into the central influence of the supra-theoretical basic-motives on the inner philosophical attitude of thought. Therefore the radical transcendental critique of theoretical thought, which I have developed in these two lectures, is, in my opinion, of a universal value for all students of philosophy. For the three transcendental basic problems of philosophical thought, which it has formulated cannot be evaded by any philosopher who wishes, indeed, to think critically. The reason is that they originate in the inner nature of the theoretical attitude of thought itself, which is one and the same for every thinker.

Every philosophical current should try to solve

them from its own starting-point, but this starting-point should no longer be camouflaged by the multi-vocal dogma concerning the autonomy of theoretical thought.

The first result of a participation of all philosophical trends in the radical transcendental criticism of theoretical thought will be that it paves the way for a real discussion between philosophers who have a different starting-point, or who have arrived at polarly opposed positions while rooted in the same dialectical basic motive. Those who participate in such a discussion should penetrate to each other's supra-theoretical presuppositions, in order to be able to exercise a truly immanent criticism of each other's philosophical views. Then they will also be prepared to learn from one another by testing their divergent philosophical conceptions of the empirical world by the real states of affairs within the structural order of human experience, which order is a common condition of every philosophy.

The continual confrontation of the different philosophical views of experience with these structural data on the one hand, and with the supra-theoretical starting points on the other, will introduce a new critical mind of mutual understanding into the philosophical debate.

One of the first structural data of human experience within the order of time which our new critique of theoretical thought has brought to light, is the fundamental modal diversity of this experience and the inter-relation of the different experiential modes.

But why should philosophers who disagree think this critique useful? —unless they believe in God?

Utopia! Seems to under-estimate rebellion of sinners.

What exactly is new in this? It is not clear.

It is true that my explanation of this structural state of affairs was from the very beginning ruled by my transcendental basic Idea which implied the mutual irreducibility of the experiential modes, in their very interrelation. And it is also true that this transcendental Idea is in turn ruled by the biblical basic motive, which unmasks, in principle, every absolutization of a relative mode of the temporal order.

But this does not detract from the fact that my transcendental view of the mutual relation between the fundamental modes of experience is capable of verification by those who do not share my starting-point. This verification may occur by confronting this view with states of affairs relating to the general basic concepts of the different special sciences, which imply a theoretical synthesis of the logical and the different non-logical experiential modes. These basic concepts contain, undoubtedly, analogical moments in which the inner coherence of the different modes of experience finds expression. From a logical positivistic standpoint this state of affairs has even led to the suggestion of a unification of the basic concepts of the different special sciences.

However, as soon as we try to reduce a fundamental experiential mode to another, our theoretical thought is entangled in unsolvable antinomies.

Some of these antinomies were already known in ancient Greek thought. I refer, for instance, to the antinomies which arise from the attempt to reduce the experiential mode of extensive movement to the spatial mode of experience. Extensive movement implies a spatial analogy, namely, that of extension. But this extensive movement is qualified by the nuclear moment of the aspect of movement, namely, that of continuous flowing, while spatial extension is of a static character.

The antinomies which result in theoretical thought from disregarding the irreducible nature of the fundamental experiential modes, show that there are structural states of affairs in our experience which cannot be neglected with impunity.

These states of affairs can, indeed, furnish a common basis for every philosophical discussion since they are transcendental data and as such have a general validity for every philosophy.

In the new critique of philosophical thought, whose principal traits I explained in these two lectures, the tracing of theoretical antinomies has been elaborated into a systematical method of immanent criticism of the philosophical systems. This method may be used to test every philosophical total view of our experiential horizon by the structural data of the latter within the temporal order.

Naturally this immanent criticism is not able to put an end to the contest between the different philosophical views of human experience and empirical reality. The reason is that the structural data meant above are liable to different philosophical interpretations in accordance with the different transcendental basic ideas which lie at the foundation of the latter. As a result even the antinomies may be philosophically interpreted in a different sense. Those who ignore the fundamental modal diversity of the temporal order of experience and hold to the autonomy of theoretical human reason in its Humanistic sense, may try to reduce them to merely logical contradictions. In his *Critique of Pure Reason* Kant, too, did so.

The central influence of the different religious basic motives upon philosophical thought is here clearly revealed. It was the very aim of our transcendental critique to show why this ultimate difference cannot be eliminated from the philosophical discussion. And I think the factual state of affairs such as it presents itself in the average debate between the different philosophical trends corroborates the results of this critique.

Does this mean that we should abandon the belief in a transcendental standard of truth which has general validity with respect to the philosophical total views of our experiential horizon and of the empirical world? Does, in other words, our transcendental critique of philosophical thought result in a general theoretical relativism by making the philosophical standard of truth dependent upon the different transcendental basis Ideas? This would be a fundamental misunderstanding of the real intention of this criticism.

The structural temporal order of our experience, to which our critique continually appealed, cannot be dependent upon the subjective transcendental basic Ideas, since it is a transcendental condition of philosophical thought itself. We have emphatically established that every state of affairs which is founded in this order, is a transcendental datum for every philosophical theory and that each philosophical total view of experience is to be tested by these data. It is true that the latter may be interpreted in different philosophical ways; but this does not mean that the philosophical interpretations are withdrawn from a general standard of truth.

These philosophical interpretations turn out to be misinterpretations insofar as they amount to a reasoning away of structural data of our experience. Such a reasoning away may originate from the love of a closed and consistently carried through philosophical system. This is a danger to which every philosopher is liable, irrespective of his religious starting-point. It shows the necessity of a really critical discussion between the different philosophical trends. But it may also be that the disregarding of essential transcendental data of our experience is caused by the religious basic motive of a philosophical school which prompts philosophical thought to absolutizations as long as it is in its central grip.

This is why the transcendental standard of truth, which is bound to the temporal structural order of our experience, is dependent on the transcendent, religious standard by which alone the central starting points of philosophy can be tested.

This really absolute standard of truth is not to be found in man, but only in the Word of God, in its central sense, which uncovers the source of all absolutizations and which alone can lead man to true knowledge of himself and of his absolute Origin.

The Sense of History
and the Historicistic World
and Life View—I

At great turning-points of world-history, man's historical consciousness is strongly aroused. The relativity of our traditional measures and opinions manifests itself in a clear way. Those who had considered them the firm ground of their personal and societal life and do not live by the Word of God can then easily fall prey to a state of spiritual uprooting, in which they surrender themselves to a radical relativism, which has lost all faith in an absolute truth.

If this state of uprooting remains restricted to a transitional phase and does not consolidate into a mass-phenomenon which finds expression in a consistently carried through life and world view, it may be soon overcome. But when it turns out to have a deeper cause than the breakdown of the belief in tradition and to be the result of a process of increasing undermining of the ultimate spiritual fundamentals of a whole civilization, we may rightly speak of a fundamental crisis of the latter.

One of the most alarming symptoms of the beginning of a fundamental crisis of Western culture since the last decades of the 19th century was the rise of a radically historicistic world and life view. This view leaves no other perspective than a spiritual nihilism, whose motto is: "Let us eat and drink, for tomorrow we die."

Radical historicism makes the historical viewpoint the all-encompassing one, absorbing all the other aspects of the human experiential horizon. Even the religious center of human experience, the human ego or selfhood, is reduced to a flowing stream of historical moments of consciousness. All our scientific, philosophical, ethical, aesthetic, political and religious standards and conceptions are viewed as the expression of the mind of a particular culture or civilization. Each civilization has arisen and ripened in the all-embracing stream of historical development. Once its florescence has ended, it is destined to decline. And it is merely dogmatical illusion to think that man would be able to view his world and life from another standpoint than the historical. History has no windows looking out into eternity. Man is completely enclosed in it and cannot elevate himself to a suprahistorical level of contemplation. History is the be-all and end-all of man's existence and of his faculty of experience. And it is ruled by destiny, the inescapable fate.

This was the radical historicism developed in Oswald Spengler's famous work, *The Decline of the West*. According to him, our Western culture is doomed to decline, and nothing can save it, since it has finished its fatal course in history. This work, published soon after the end of the first world-war and written in a brilliant style, made a deep impression. In many respects it prepared the way for the flood-tide of the so-called existentialistic, philosophical movement, which acquired a dominant position in European thought, especially since the last world-war. In existentialism, the historicistic view is exclusively concentrated upon the human selfhood in its position in the world. But the basic pessimistic tone of Spengler's view of human, historical existence is clearly maintained. Destiny, concern and anxiety, death and human failure, night without dawn, these are the ruling themes of this philosophy, in so far as it held to a purely historicistic viewpoint. Toynbee's voluminous work on world-history also clearly reveals the influence of Spengler's ideas. However, it may be observed, that this English writer tries to break through Spengler's fatalism by positing his expectation of an ultimate revival of true Christendom in a non-dogmatic, syncretist sense. Such a revival alone, according to Toynbee, will be able to save Western culture from its destiny of decline.

It should be noticed that from the outset Historicism did not display that radical character, which we observe in Spengler. It originated in the first decennaries of the last century, in the period of the so-called Restoration. Many leading thinkers of that period opposed the historical mode of thought to the mathematical and natural science pattern of thinking, which had ruled the philosophical picture of world and life in the preceding period since Descartes. To speak more exactly, we should say that the rise of a moderate historicism dates from the first decennaries of the 18th century. In fact, it was the Italian philosopher Vico, who was the first to set the historical model of science in opposition to the mathematical Cartesian science ideal. However, the historicistic world-view in general did not gain ground over against the anti-historical world-picture of the preceding period until the time of the Restoration.

What was the background of this opposition? Modern philosophy, founded by the French thinker, Descartes, had a hidden starting-point, which was radically different from that of the medieval scholastic philosophy of Thomas Aquinas. The latter had been accepted as the rational foundation of the Roman Catholic doctrine. But the Cartesian philosophy, though its founder sought to avoid every direct conflict with the church, was in fact ruled by the religious basic motive of the Humanistic movement, which has arisen since the Italian Renaissance. This Renaissance was, in the first place, a religious movement, aiming at a transformation of the Christian religion into a religion of the human personality and of humanity. It required a real rebirth of man, not in its biblical sense, but in the sense of his regeneration into a completely free and autonomous personality, the sole ruler of his own destiny and that of the world. The central biblical theme of creation, fall into sin, and redemption by Jesus Christ in the communion of the Holy Spirit, was indeed reinterpreted in the sense of this Humanistic freedom-motive. Relying on his natural reason alone, man supposedly could recreate his world and his god in his own image. This Copernican revolution, which the Humanistic freedom-motive brought about in the biblical view of man's creation in the image of God, called up a new religious view of nature as the macrocosmic reflected image of the free and emancipated human personality. The "discovery of nature" by the Renaissance man brought about a new religious attitude towards the world, which also needed liberation from the ecclesiastical view of creation, sin and miracles.

This central religious basic motive of modern Humanism may be correctly designated as that of nature and freedom. Since the famous German philosopher, Immanuel Kant, this denomination has generally been accepted, to indicate the central theme which ruled the Humanist world and life view, but which in fact was its religious starting point. This motive was radically different from that of medieval scholastic philosophy since Thomas Aquinas, namely, that of nature and supra-natural grace. This latter meant that there is a natural sphere in creation, which can be known by the natural light of human reason alone, but that this sphere is subordinated to a supra-natural sphere of grace, which is only to be known by divine revelation, entrusted to the Church. Therefore, natural reason should not contradict the supra-natural truths of the doctrine of the Church, so that medieval philosophy was subjected to ecclesiastical control.

This scholastic motive of nature and grace, which entered the Roman Catholic doctrine, deprived the central theme of the Word-revelation, namely that of creation, fall into sin and redemption by Jesus Christ in the communion of the Holy Spirit, of its radical and integral character. By accepting a natural sphere of life, which was supposed to be related to the human intellect alone apart from any religious presupposition, it paved the way for a philosophy which did not acknowledge any other authority than human reason.

Humanist philosophy eliminated the so-called supra-natural sphere. Nor would it accept a given world-order, founded in the divine creation. This was incompatible with its religious basic-motive, which implied the absolute autonomy of human reason. It could not accept any order of the world that does not originate from the autonomous and free human reason itself. Therefore, the Cartesian philosophy started with a methodical, theoretical destruction of the world as it presents itself in the given order of human experience. After this methodical destruction of the given world, the thinking human ego, with its innate mathematical ideas, alone is left. And this thinking ego, which seeks the criterion of truth in itself alone, sets itself the task of recreating the world in the image of its mathematical pattern of thought.

We meet with the same Humanist transformation of the biblical idea of creation in the philosophy of Descartes' younger British contemporary, Thomas Hobbes. In the foreword of his work, *De Corpore* (on the corporeal world) , in which he explains his philos-

ophy of nature, he says that philosophy should begin
with a methodical destruction of the given world.
With a clear allusion to the first chapter of the book
of Genesis, he suggests that after this methodical
experiment logical thought should command: "Let
there be light!" And this allusion is corroborated by
the following explanation: "For logical thought
should create, like God or like the artist."

To achieve this rule of the world of nature by
creative, autonomous thought alone, both Descartes
and Hobbes projected a picture of the world after a
strictly mathematical and mechanical pattern. This
picture of nature did not leave any room for the
autonomous freedom of man in his practical activity
within the world. For, as a corporeal, natural being
man was supposed to be subjected to the same mechanical causality, which ruled this image of nature
as a whole. To save human freedom, which was
supposed to have its center in mathematical thought,
Descartes suggested that the human soul, conceived
as a thinking substance, should be considered philosophically as if no body existed, and vice versa. But
Hobbes did not acknowledge this limitation of the
mechanical world-image. The rational soul, too,
should be considered as a mechanism.

So the Humanist basic motive of nature and freedom began to display its inner conflict and dialectical
tension. The mechanistic idol of nature, evoked by
the Humanist freedom-motive itself, turned out to be
a true Leviathan (the legendary monster mentioned
in the book of Job), which threatened to devour the

idol of the free and autonomous human personality.

This conflict was, consequently, not of a merely theoretical, philosophical character. Rather, it originated in the central religious starting-point of Humanist thought. Hence it did not allow for a real solution, from the Humanist standpoint. The only way out was the ascription of the primacy, or the religious precedence, to one of the two opposing motives, either to that of the rule over nature, or to that of practical human freedom; with the result, naturally, that the other was depreciated.

The continual shifting of the primacy from the one motive to the other caused a dialectical process in modern Humanistic thought, which drove it in polarly opposite directions, from the naturalistic pole to that of freedom-idealism, and vice versa. The ascription of the primacy to the nature-motive meant, indeed, a cult of mathematical and natural scientific thought, which was supposed to be capable of creating an image of nature as it really is, in contradistinction to that which presents itself in the given order of human experience. The cult of this science-ideal implied also an idea of the divine creator, constructed in the image of this pattern of thought. For this reason the great German philosopher, Leibnitz, called God the great Geometer.

His discovery of differential and integral calculus called up in his religious consciousness the idol of a divine mathematician able to carry through this admirable method of mathematical analysis to such an extent that it would even make calculable the chance occurrences.

So long as this mathematical science-ideal had the primacy in modern philosophy, even human society was constructed after its pattern. The given societal order, which still showed many remnants of the medieval feudal regime, did not satisfy the Humanist view of human autonomy. Thus, this societal order, too, was subjected to a methodical destruction by theoretical thought. It was dissolved into its supposed elemental components, the free and equal individuals who were assumed to have existed in a pre-societal state of nature. From these elements philosophical thought could freely create a theoretical image of human society corresponding to the Humanist mathematical science-ideal, which aims at complete control over the temporal world.

The first concern was to construct a body politic, provided with absolute power over all other societal relationships, in order to dissolve all connection with medieval society. To this end, the state was defined as an artificial body characterized by its absolute sovereignty, excluding any internal sphere sovereignty of non-political institutions such as the family and the church. To make this absolute sovereignty acceptable, it was adapted to the Humanist idea of the autonomous freedom of man, by the construction of a general and reciprocal social contract between individuals, whether or not this was accompanied by a second contract with the instituted sovereign government. By this compact the individuals were supposed to have abandoned their natural freedom by their own autonomous will and to have transferred all power to the instituted sovereign government. The validity of this compact was derived from a natural law principle: namely, that agreements are to be kept, which was assumed to be founded in the autonomous human reason.

Notwithstanding this formal concession, however, to the Humanist freedom-ideal, it was clear that the State Leviathan, construed after the mathematical pattern of thought, absorbed all human freedom. Here, too, the inner conflict in the Humanist basic motive of nature and freedom was clearly revealed. Political theory, the theory of law, and the entire view of human society was, in this period, quite anti-historical.

The supremacy of the mathematical science-ideal could not fail to call forth a strong reaction on the part of the threatened freedom-motive. The shifting of the religious primacy to the latter motive had already announced itself in the 18th century, in a fundamental criticism of Cartesian philosophy, and in the rise of the doctrine of innate and inalienable human rights and of the liberal state-idea, which were both developed by John Locke. Rousseau openly discounted the mathematical science-ideal and proclaimed the absolute precedence of the ideal of practical human freedom. Kant, who was strongly influenced by him, depreciated the scientific image of nature by restricting it to the world of sense phenomena. According to him, freedom and volitional autonomy of the human personality do not belong to the world of nature but to the supra-sensory kingdom of ethics, which does not relate to what *is* but what *ought to be*. Human freedom is an idea of the practical reason, which can neither be proved, nor refuted by scientific thought, since the latter is restricted to the sensory world of nature. One should believe in the freedom of human personality, since our practical reason commands us to do so, and practical reason has the absolute primacy.

This shifting of the primacy to the freedom-motive requires, as its correlate, also a Humanist idea of God. The Kantian god is no longer the divine Geometer. Rather he has become the deified image of the autonomous and free human personality in its ethical aspect. The idea of God is, according to Kant, a requirement of the practical human reason, that is to say, of an autonomous ethics. There ought to be a God, able to recompense human virtue with eternal beatitude, since in the present life moral human freedom and autonomy can only be realized at the cost of man's natural happiness.

Thus the inner conflict between the nature-motive and the freedom-motive in the religious starting-point of Humanism led Kant to a strongly dualistic world and life view. Nature and freedom were sharply separated from one another. And this separation corresponded to Kant's separation between science and faith, which consequently had a religious background. But the ascription of the religious primacy to the freedom-motive did not immediately give rise to another pattern of scientific thought instead of the mathematical and natural scientific view of Descartes and Hobbes. So long as the individualistic and rationalistic view of human personality in its social relationships was not abandoned, the influence of the mathematical science-ideal was not completely overcome. Both Rousseau and Kant continued to construct human society, in a mathematical way, from its supposed elements, namely, the abstract human individuals, in their presumed natural freedom and equality.

The rationalistic trait in Kantian ethics, testifying to the continued influence of the mathematical science-ideal upon him, comes to the fore in his conception of the autonomy of man's ethical will. The true *autos*, i. e., selfhood of man, is, according to him, identical with the general formula of the *nomos*, i. e., the ethical law (categorical imperative), which his practical reason prescribes to him. The pure ethical will was supposed to have no other motivation than respect for this general law. There was no room left for the individuality of the human person in this legalistic ethics. As an abstract individual every person was considered to be nothing but a specimen of this general normative idea of human personality.

Therefore Kant lacked the insight into a real community as a social whole, which is not identical with the sum of the individuals, but brings about an inner inter-relation between its members.

However, in the period of the Restoration, after the liquidation of the French Revolution, the Humanistic freedom-motive began to reveal itself in a new version of the development of the post-Kantian

idealistic philosophy. The Kantian belief in the
eternal normative idea of a free and autonomus mankind was maintained. But the legalistic view of the
ideal human personality, willing to conform himself
to the general rule of the ethical law, was rejected.
It is no longer the general law which determines the
true selfhood of man, but the reverse is true. The
ethical rule of behavior can only be derived from
the concrete individuality of the human personality,
from its individual disposition and task in the world.
This was the irrationalistic counter-part of Kant's
rationalistic view of human autonomy. Rationalism
seeks to eliminate the irreducible individuality of the
human subject by reducing its true selfhood to a
general law of man's practical reason. The irrationalistic view, on the contrary, rejects every general law
as a falsification of true reality, and it absolutizes the
incomparable subjective individuality of human
personality.

To evade the anarchical consequences of this ethical
irrationalism, Romanticism and post-Kantian idealism bound it to the idea of human community, especially to the idea of the national community, which
had strongly come to the foreground in the Napole-
onic wars. This meant that the Humanist freedom
idea was now applied to man in national community.
Abstract individuals, so it was argued, do not exist.
Every man is born into the community of a nation,
which determines his individual character; while the
communal will at the same time determines man's
own autonomous will. The nation is a temporal reve-

lation of the eternal idea of humanity, of a spiritual community. Every nation has its own individual mind, its *Volksgeist*. It brings forth its own culture in autonomous, creative freedom, inclusive of its own political organization, its own language, its own customs, its own legal order, its own fine arts, and so forth. General patterns of political constitutions and law, of moral and aesthetic standards, et cetera, which are suitable to every people and to every time, as the rationalistic philosophy of the French Revolution imagined, do not exist. The individual national mind creates its culture including all its social institutions and rules, in a long process of historical development.

This development is one of autonomous freedom without being arbitrary. On the contrary, it has creative power, which operates in conformity to a hidden natural necessity, so that the historical development of a national culture is an organic process, which is sharply distinguished from all revolutionary mechanical and artificial modes of cultural fabrication.

What does it mean that the process of historical development is conceived here as a combination of autonomous freedom and natural necessity?

Post-Kantian idealism was not satisfied with Kant's critical separation between nature and freedom. It sought to overcome the inner conflict in the religious starting-point of Humanism by a so-called dialectical mode of thought, which was supposed to bring about a synthesis between the opposite motives of nature and freedom. To do this, the mathematical and mechanical image of nature, constructed by the Cartesian philosophy, had to be abandoned. The famous German philosopher, Schelling, proclaimed the identity of nature and the free spirit as two forms of appearance of the absolute. Nature should be viewed after the pattern of a living organism, developing itself into many forms from different potencies. He conceived of the organic process of nature as developing into ever higher forms as the unconscious operation of the world-spirit, whose free creative power works at the same time as a natural necessity. This organic development of nature is continued on a higher level in the historical development of the national minds, conceived as the spiritual potencies of human culture. In this historical process the creative freedom of the nations manifests itself also in conformity to a natural necessity which gives to this process an organical character. It is the individual nature of a nation which unfolds itself with this inner necessity. History does not know general laws. Nevertheless, there lies a hidden law at the foundation of the organic development of a culture. As a gift of Providence, every national mind contains the *Schicksal,* or destiny of the national culture which originates from it.

The founders of the historical school, having been thoroughly influenced by this romanticist world-view, began to develop a new historical pattern of scientific thought, which was sharply opposed to the mathematical and mechanistic thought mode of natural science. This new model of thought was applied in jurisprudence, political theory, economics, aesthetics and linguistics. After this pattern they designed a historicistic image of reality, which soon was generally accepted as an axiom. Even many leading Christian thinkers and politicians welcomed this historicistic view, especially in its application to human society, as a powerful ally in their contest against the principles of the French Revolution. They did not realize that this historicism was rooted in the same humanistic religious basic motive, which had also ruled the philosophic ideas of Rousseau and his revolutionary disciples.

But we should not lose sight of the fact that the radical consequences of this new view of reality could not yet reveal themselves so long as they were checked by the firm belief in eternal values or ideas, which realize themselves in the temporal order of the historical process in a wealth of individual national forms. Thus it is understandable that the Christian thinkers who joined the Historical School were of the opinion that this view was more biblical than the rationalistic philosophy of the fathers of the French Revolution. What else, so they argued, is the Bible, than the revelation of God's eternal plan in history?

Especially the irrationalistic view that the organic development of history occurs in accordance with a hidden Providence, seemed to be quite congenial to the Christian belief in God's guidance in history. This hidden law of history could not fail to be interpreted in an irrationalistic normative sense as a rule for human behavior. And it was the Lutheran legal philosopher, Fr. Julius Stahl, who openly accepted this conclusion. In his opinion all that has come to pass in the long process of historical development, under the influence of incalculable and inscrutable forces, without the interference of rational human planning, ought to be respected as a manifestation of God's guidance in history, inasfar as it does not contradict God's revealed law.

This view of God's providence in history was quite in accordance with the conservative mind of the Restoration, and it had a great influence upon the whole so-called Christian-historical, or anti-revolutionary movement in Germany, the Netherlands and France. Stahl, too, had a strong belief in eternal ideas, which he conceived in a christianized sense as ideas of the divine world-order realizing themselves in history.

But the historicist world-picture had the inner tendency to undermine this belief. As soon as the idealistic philosophy which had created it, broke down, the historicist mode of thought began in an increasing degree to reveal its radical consequences. What else, so it was argued, is human belief itself than the historical product of a particular mind of culture? What else are the so-called eternal ideas but ideas derived from our Western civilization, reflecting the particular course of its historical development.

Nevertheless, as long as the development of Western civilization continued to be considered the center and standard of world-history, the radical form of historicism, which we meet with in Oswald Spengler, was out of the question. For this view, which was common both to the historical philosophy of the period of

Enlightenment and to that of the post-Kantian freedom-idealism, implied the firm belief in a particular historical vocation of Western culture. This vocation would imply that in the process of its development this civilization would reach an ultimate stage, in which the final aim of the entire world-history would be realized. And this final aim itself was withdrawn from the historicistic relativizing of all measures and values. The belief in either a steady, straight-lined, or in a dialectically conceived progress of mankind in its historical development, was inherent in this view.

And even after its emancipation from the idealistic philosophy, the historicistic picture of the world and life remained in general checked by this belief, until the break-down of this belief announced the fundamental crisis of Western civilization. Henceforth, Western culture was no longer viewed as the center of world-history, but as a particular civilization on the same footing with the Arabian, the Indian, Chinese and other cultures.

Meanwhile, the transition from the inconsistent to the consistent, or radical, historicism was only a question of time. This transition started as soon as the idealistic foundation of the historical mode of thought was itself submitted to an historical explanation. The French thinker, August Comte, the founder of modern sociology, was the first to subject both the Christian belief and the Humanistic belief in the so-called eternal ideas of human reason to the historicistic view. With him the idealistic philosophical position was replaced by a positivistic one. This meant, in fact, the restoration of the supremacy of the natural scientific mode of thought, but in such a way that the new historicistic view of human society was retained. The latter should only be adapted to the general pattern of natural scientific research which seeks to explain the empirical facts by tracing the general laws of their causal inter-relations.

Thus Comte attempted to trace the general law of the social history of mankind. And he clearly realized that this attempt was ruled by the old Humanistic motive to dominate both nature and the social world by autonomous scientific thought. So he formulated his famous law of the three stages. According to it, human history proceeds from a theological to a metaphysical stage, and from the latter to a positivistic one. Each of them is ruled by particular ideas, corresponding to a particular type of society. The theological ideas, inclusive of Christian doctrine, must necessarily give place to the metaphysical ideas. The latter includes both, the supposed eternal ideas of the rationalistic Humanist doctrine of natural law and those of its antipode, the idealistic metaphysics of history. These, in turn, are necessarily to be overcome by the positivistic, or scientific man.

But this historicistic relativizing of the belief in eternal ideas was not yet carried through in a radical sense. For the last stage of human history is, according to Comte, the very aim of the entire historical process, the stage of a new humanity, which in complete freedom and autonomy rules the world, and has developed to the highest level of social solidarity, welfare and

morality, supplemented with a new Humanistic religion. In other words, Comte held to a strong belief
in the future of mankind. The ideas of his positivistic
philosophy, arisen in the development of Western
civilization, are to his mind, of a really eternal value. And the idea of the steady and straight-lined
progress of mankind by the autonomous power of
science, which was characteristic of the period of the
Enlightenment, lay at the foundation of his entire
view of history.

Marxism, the source of contemporary Communism,
gave to the idealistic and dialectical historicistic
world-view of Hegel a materialistic turn. According
to Marx, all human ideas, inclusive of the religious
doctrines are nothing but the ideological reflection of
a particular technical system of economic production,
which arises, ripens and breaks down in the course of
history with an inner dialectical necessity.

Nevertheless, Marx was no more radical a historicist
than was Comte. For, he too was committed strongly
to the belief in an eschatological consummation of
history; the final redemption and liberation of mankind by the suffering proletariat, which will found
an earthly paradise of a classless communistic society,
after the destruction of capitalism. This Humanistic
transformation of the Messianic faith became the
gospel of international communism, which founded
its Jerusalem in Moscow, after the Russian revolution.

However, the radical Historicism, which began to
undermine the spiritual fundamentals of our Western
civilization since the last decades of the 19th century,

has not retained any positive belief. The famous German philosopher and historian, Wilhelm Dilthey, who in many respects was one of its most brilliant apostles, said that it would lead humanity to the highest level of freedom, since it liberates our mind from the last remnants of dogmatical prejudices. But at his seventieth birthday he added something to this eulogy, which clearly testified to his fear of the nihilistic apparition, which he had evoked. "Yes," said he, "historicism has freed the mind from the last remnants of dogmatism. But who will check the radical relativism, which it has brought forth?"

Historicism, whose rise and evolution we have briefly sketched, appears to exercise a magical influence upon those who have come under its spell. From the very beginning it displayed a strongly aesthetical trait. Schelling ascribed to the entire process of history an aesthetical aim, namely, the production of the perfect work of fine art, in which nature and creative freedom were supposed to find their ultimate synthesis.

We have also seen that in its initial irrationalistic form the historicistic view captivated many Christian thinkers. But it should be noted that it is exactly the irrationalistic current in Historicism which, since the breakdown of the Humanist freedom-idealism, has resulted in the radical relativism of Spengler and his followers. The rationalistic trend, in the footsteps of August Comte, sought to trace general laws of history. This view, which found many adherents in Anglo-Saxon countries, never has carried through the historistic view to its ultimate conclusions. However, the rationalistic form of historicism, in general did not attract Christian thinkers, but it rather repelled them, especially since it joined with Darwinian evolutionism.

This should prompt us to ask the question: "What is the snare in the historicistic view of our temporal world in both of its forms?" And, "what is the real place and meaning of the historical aspect in the temporal order of our experience?" We shall try to answer these questions in our second lecture on this subject.

The Sense of History
and the Historicistic World
and Life View—II

In the previous lecture I tried to give you a brief outline of the development of modern Historicism and its spiritual background. If the historicistic view is restricted to our temporal world and is not turned against the supra-temporal, religious sphere of truth, it seems, at first sight, quite acceptable from the Christian viewpoint.

But our critical doubt as to its tenability is aroused when we consider that it is a philosophical total-view of empirical reality within the temporal order of our experiential horizon. And this total view originated from the absolutization of the scientific historical viewpoint. As such it is nothing but one of the many isms in the philosophical views of reality. It is on the same footing as the others, such as mechanism, biologism, psychologism, logicism, aestheticism, moralism, et cetera.

All these *isms* originate from the absolutizing of a specific scientific viewpoint which considers empirical reality only from one of the fundamental aspects of our temporal experience. These aspects are the fundamental *modes* or *manners* of this experience. As such they are only related to the *how* of the latter, not to the concrete *what,* i.e., to concrete things, or events, or particular societal relationships, which we experience in these different modes or aspects. This concrete *what,* e. g., the battle of Waterloo, is never to be identified with one of its aspects. It is an individual whole, which in principle functions in all the aspects of our experience.

The different modes or aspects of our experiential horizon are arranged in an irreversible order and display an unbreakable mutual coherence. It is only in the theoretical or scientific attitude of thought that we separate them and set them in opposition to one another. And we do so in order to delimit the different specific scientific viewpoints from which empirical reality is considered and examined.

In the non-theoretical and pre-scientific attitude of thought and experience we never do so. Here our attention is directed immediately upon concrete things and events as individual wholes; and their different aspects are only experienced implicitly, not in the way of a theoretical logical distinction.

If in the pre-scientific attitude of experience, we try to answer the question: "What is history?" we usually say: "That which has happened in the past." From this non-theoretical experiential attitude this answer is doubtless correct. Here we do not reflect on the particular historical mode of our experience, but we give our attention exclusively to the concrete *what,* which is experienced in this way. And so we refer to the concrete events that have occurred in the past.

But if we wish to acquire an insight into the historical viewpoint, which in principle delimits the scientific field of research in historiography, there is no use in referring to the concrete *what,* that is experienced in the historical way. We are then much rather interested in this particular mode of experience itself, that is to say, in the historical aspect of our experience as such. If I drank a cup of coffee yesterday and smoked a cigar, these facts belong to the past today. But are these activities really historical facts, are they of any concern to the historian? They are, as such, certainly not historical facts in a typical sense. That is, they are not facts which are typically qualified by their historical aspect, such as the battle of Waterloo, the invention of typography, or, the great invasion of the Allied military forces in France during the last world-war.

Nevertheless, such simple things as drinking and smoking certainly have an historical aspect. In the Middle Ages one did not drink coffee or smoke cigars. The introduction of these means of enjoyment into our Western civilization has doubtless influenced our cultural life in an historical sense.

But what is the historical aspect of the facts concerned? The historians themselves, insofar as they are not interested in the epistemological problems of their branch of science, are not able to answer the question concerning the specific nature of their scientific viewpoint. Their attention is only directed upon the historical facts in their historical context, i. e., upon the concrete *what* presenting itself within the historical aspect of our experience.

Nevertheless, it is only from this aspect that they consider their scientific material. This means that they, indeed, abstract this aspect from the full reality of the facts as we experience them in life. The great German historian, Leopold Ranke, answered the question as to the manner of procedure in historiography as follows: "I describe how it has truly been." This answer was certainly somewhat naive, since no single science is able to examine the full empirical reality of events. Other historians have said that their scientific approach is the genetical one. The science of history then is the science of becoming, or evolution. But every empirical science has its own genetical viewpoint, and consequently uses the term evolution, or becoming, in a different sense. Therefore, this term in itself is not defined in its meaning. It is of an analogical, or multivocal character.

What distinguishes the genetical viewpoint of the historian from that of the geologist or biologist or psychologist is exactly its historical character, which we are seeking for. Consequently, it cannot be the genetical viewpoint of the historian which determines the historical mode of experience, but the reverse is true. How can we explain that the meaning of the terms evolution, development, or becoming varies with the different scientific viewpoints from which empirical reality is approached?

Every aspect of our experiential horizon, as a

fundamental manner or mode of experience, has a modal structure, in which the whole temporal order and mutual coherence of the different aspects finds its inner expression. This modal structure displays a nuclear moment, which guarantees the irreducible proper meaning of the aspect concerned. But this modal kernel can unfold this meaning only in an un- breakable context with a series of so-called analogical moments. These latter refer backward or forward, respectively, to the modal kernels of the aspects which have either an earlier or a later place in the temporal order of experience.

In conformity to this different direction of their reference, we distinguish the analogical moments into retrospective and anticipatory ones. Their specific meaning is always determined by the nuclear moment of the experiential aspect in which they function. From this it follows that only an exact analysis of the modal structure of the historical aspect of our expe- rience can bring to light both the proper meaning of this experiential mode and its place in the temporal order of the aspects.

The historicistic view of the temporal world could not absolutize the historical aspect of our experience without eliminating its modal structure. For it is this very structure which excludes in principle any at- tempt at reducing all the other modes of experience to mere modalities of the historical. The proper sense of the latter can only reveal itself in an unbreakable context with that of the other aspects. And this state of affairs explains why a consistent or radical historicism must lead to nihilism, which denies any meaning to history. For the absolutizing of a particular aspect, whose meaning is only relative, destroys this meaning and accordingly results in utter meaninglessness.

To strike Historicism in its vitals, we must try to trace the modal kernel of the historical mode of experience. What is this irreducible nuclear moment of its structure?

An etymological inquiry into the term "history" itself cannot help us to detect it. This word is of Greek origin and had initially no other meaning than investigation.

This neutral sense revealed itself also in the use of the term *natural* history, which acquired a particular signification only since Romanticist philosophy and Darwinian evolutionism, which used it in a direct context with the history of mankind. It was the analogical, i. e., the in itself multivocal concept of evolution or development, which served as a kind of a basic denominator for the so-called natural history as well as for history in its proper use.

Nevertheless, even from the historicistic standpoint it was necessary to indicate a criterion for the distinction between the fields of research of historiography proper and that of the natural sciences which are concerned with the examination of natural history in its genetic sense.

Now, all modern philosophical attempts at delimiting the proper historical scientific viewpoint from that of the genetic natural sciences, resulted in accepting the notion of culture as the central criterion.

But what was understood by culture? Here the influence of the religious basic motive of Humanistic thought which I have explained in my first lecture, clearly manifested itself. The Italian philosopher, Vico, who was the first to set the historical mode of thought over against the mathematical and scientific one, identified culture with human society which he called the civil world. In clear opposition to the Cartesian point of view, he said that it is not nature which is created by human reason, but only the civil world of human culture.

Naturally, Descartes had not pretended that properly speaking nature is created by human thought. It was only the mathematical and mechanistic picture of nature which was viewed as an autonomous creation of methodical mathematical thought. Vico, however, set himself against this mechanistic world-picture from the standpoint of the Humanist freedom-motive. According to him the true creative freedom of human reason does not reveal itself in mathematical and natural scientific thought, but in the creation of the cultural world of human society. And this creation occurs in an historical process by the rational mind of the nations. Human culture, as a result of this creative process, embraces all that in human social life surpasses the animal level of existence; the social institutions of marriage and family, the political institutions, the forms of conventional social intercourse, language, economy, fine arts, law, morality, religion. In this way culture was viewed as a second world in addition to the world of nature, a world of a specific historical reality. And the principles of its social order were supposed to be found in practical human reason as the creator of this civil world.

This identification of culture with the whole of man's societal world maintained itself in all the later philosophical theories of history. It was the very basis of the historicistic world-view, which originated in an absolutization of the historical aspect of human experience. Every ism in the realm of philosophical world-views, begins with the identification of a particular aspect or mode of experience with the full reality of our empirical world. In this way a really critical analysis of the notion of culture was excluded in principle.

A reality of a purely cultural character cannot exist. It is the noun-form of the word *culture,* which has favored this misconception, just as the noun-form of the term *life* has favored the identification of reality with the biological mode of experience, which led to the vitalistic, or biologistic world-view. We shall, therefore, replace the noun *culture* with the adjective *cultural,* in order to emphasize that it is only a modal aspect of our temporal world which is meant. Taken in this modal sense, the term "cultural" means nothing but a particular (experiential) mode of formation, or moulding, which is fundamentally different from all modes of formation found in nature and conceived in the physico-chemical or biotic aspects of experience. It is a controlling mode whereby form is given to a material according to a freely elaborate and variable plan.

A spider spins its web with faultless precision; but it does so after a fixed and uniform pattern prescribed by the instinct of the species. It lacks free control or dominion over its material, which is the very condition of the variability of all cultural formation. Thus the cultural mode of formation must receive its specific qualification through freedom of control, domination or power. This is why the great cultural commandment given to man at creation reads: "Subdue the earth and have dominion over it."

And if the genuine historical viewpoint of historiography is that of the cultural development of humanity, it follows that formative power or control must also be the modal kernel of the historical aspect. It is this nuclear moment, which alone can give the analogical or multi-vocal concept of development its proper historical sense. The historical development of mankind means in principle, then, the development of its formative power over the world and over its societal life.

The cultural mode of formation reveals itself in two directions, which are closely connected with each other. On the one hand it is a formative power over persons unfolding itself by giving cultural form to their societal existence; on the other, it appears as a controlling manner of shaping natural materials, things, or forces to cultural ends.

The Germans speak of *Personkultur* and *Sachkultur*. Since all cultural phenomena are bound to human society in its historical development, the development of *Sachkultur* is in principle dependent on that of

Personkultur. For the cultural formation of natural materials or forces can only occur by human persons, who must learn it by socio-cultural education, given in a socio-cultural form to their minds. In addition, both *Personkultur* and *Sachkultur* presuppose the leading ideas of a project, which leading figures or groups in history seek to realize in a human society. Therefore, the formative power of these leading figures and groups always implies an intentional relation to such ideas.

These ideas cannot be realized according to the merely subjective conception of those who propagate them. They must assume a socio-cultural form so that they themselves may be able to exercise formative power in the relationships of society. By way of example, I refer to the cultural influence of the ideas of natural law, especially the idea of the innate human rights, or to the cultural influence of the technological ideas of great inventors, of the aesthetic ideas of great artists, of the moral ideas of the preachers of new moralities, et cetera. Such ideas are not of a cultural historical significance in themselves; but they acquire a historical significance as soon as they begin to exercise formative power in human society. They can be realized only in typical total structures of societal relationships which in principle function in all aspects of our experiential horizon, such as a state, an industrial community, a school, a religious community, and so forth. The empirical reality of a human society can, therefore, never be exhausted in its cultural-historical aspect, as Historicism assumed. All that is real or that really happens in human society is more than merely historical.

After having established in this way the nuclear moment of the historical aspect of our experience, we may now turn to the analogical concept of *historical development.* In the previous lecture we have seen that the Historical School which in the first half of the last century introduced the new historical mode of thought into all branches of social scientific research, sharply emphasized this concept. And it is beyond doubt that it is this very notion which enables the historian to discover inner coherences in the temporal succession of historical facts and changes. It is the process of historical development which binds the present historical condition of human society to the previous phases of its history. If this notion of development would be abandoned, no single synthetic insight into a historical process would be possible, and historiography would degenerate into a collection of mixed reports from the past.

But it is exactly the analogical or multivocal character of this concept which has raised serious doubt as to its scientific significance. The famous Dutch historian, Huizinga, has asked the question whether our speaking of development in history does not rest on a mere metaphor. This word, says he, is taken from biology, where it relates to the process of evolution of a living organism. But what meaning can it have when it is transferred to history? Our answer must be that, as a biotic analogy in our cultural historical mode of experience, the notion of historical development is implied in that of socio-cultural life, which can certainly not be a mere metaphor. It is true that all other modes of life, such as the sensitive, cultural, economic, aesthetic, juridical, moral and the faith life, refer back to the original mode of organic life which is their indispensable foundation. But this does not mean that they could be reduced to the latter, or, if this turns out to be impossible, that they might be considered mere metaphors on the same footing as for instance the metaphorical use of the term "play" in the phrase: "The play of the waves." The sense of life and development is not exhausted in that of their biological mode of manifestation. Jesus Christ has said that man shall not live by bread alone, but by every word that procedes out of the mouth of God. Here the term "live" is certainly not used metaphorically, but much rather in the religious fullness of its meaning. So we must try to trace the particular meaning of historical development from the modal structure of the cultural historical aspect of experience.

We have seen that the proper meaning of a particular aspect of our experience can only reveal itself in its unbreakable coherence with that of all the other modal aspects. And this coherence of meaning finds expression in a series of analogical moments in its structure referring backward and forward respectively to all aspects which have an earlier or later place in the temporal order. This means that every analogical moment in the cultural or historical mode of experience has its particular place in the order of analogies and cannot reveal its proper cultural historical sense apart from the others.

As a biotic analogy in the cultural sense of history, cultural development refers backwards to development in its biological sense. But not directly. The historical mode of experience is immediately founded in the logical or analytical mode of distinguishing our experiences. In other words, the cultural-historical aspect is directly founded in the logical. Without the basis of logical distinction no single historical experience is possible.

Let us take for example the battle of Waterloo as a historical fact. The famous Austrian economist, Hayek, raised the question whether the work of the farmers, who tried desperately to save their crops on the battle-fields, also belonged to the battle.

This question is very instructive. For it proves that our historical mode of experiencing the battle of Waterloo cannot be founded on a record of sensory perception alone. From the sensory viewpoint the work of the farmers took place without a doubt on the battle-field. But, implicitly, we make an analytical, or logical distinction, between the action of persons, whether or not they pertain to the battle as a historical contest of power between Napoleon's forces and those of his allied opponents.

This inner coherence between the logical and the historical aspects finds expression in their modal structure. The historical aspect must consequently display logical analogies.

I shall restrict myself to indicating that logical analogy in the historical mode of experience which gives a further determination to the analogical concept of historical development. In the logical aspect of our thought and experience we meet with the fundamental logical relation of contradiction. We experience a logical contradiction when an argument avails itself of two propositions which exclude one another in a logical sense. In this case we posit that this mode of reasoning is illogical; and this statement implies a normative evaluation, since it implies the validity of a fundamental logical norm of thought which forbids such contradictions.

Now it is indisputable that in all experiential aspects which are based on the logical, an analogy of this normative logical contrast is found. This is a strong indication of the normative character of these aspects, which means that within their modes of experience behavior is not subject to laws of nature, but to norms, relating to what ought to be. I refer to the contrasts: polite-impolite, decent-indecent, and other such contrasts which function in the aspect of conventional social intercourse; to the contrast: linguistically right or wrong, which we meet with in the linguistic aspect of experience; to the contrasts: aesthetic-unaesthetic, economic-uneconomic, lawful-unlawful, moral-immoral, believing-unbelieving, which occur respectively in the aesthetic, economic, juridical, moral and in the faith aspects of our experiential horizon.

Hence, the analogical notion of historical development is unbreakably connected with the contrast historical-unhistorical, or progressive-reactionary. By this contrast we mean that the behavior or program of a leading figure or group is in line with, or contrary to the requirements of historical development. As a clear analogy of the logical relation of contradiction, this contrast implies a normative criterion, so that the concept of historical development must itself have a normative cultural meaning. And since the contrast concerned appeared to be founded in the modal structure of the historical aspect itself, its normative sense cannot be reduced to a merely subjective evaluation of the factual course of history. Rather it must be founded on an objective norm of historical development which implicitly lies at the foundation of the cultural historical mode of experience.

No one, whose historical consciousness has not been supplanted by non-historical political considerations, will deny that from a politico-historical viewpoint the so-called counter-revolutionary movement in Europe, which after the defeat of Napoleon, strove for the restoration of the medieval feudal regime, was of a reactionary character. This judgment will be independent of the question whether or not one admires the cultural forms of medieval society, and whether or not the memory of those times is recalled with a kind of romantic desire. But on what objective norm of historical development may this judgment be founded?

The German historical school made a sharp distinction between living and dead elements in the historical tradition of a nation. The former should be utilized in the progressive line of further development, the latter should be sloughed off. This was the reason that the Historical school rejected any reactionary attempt to revive the medieval political regíme.

But this school failed to produce a supra-arbitrary norm of cultural development whereby we can establish what is the proper historical meaning of the terms progress and reaction. And the reason is that its conception of historical development clings exclusively to the biotic analogies in the cultural-historical mode of experience. Taking the natural development of a living organism as a pattern, the adherents of this school stressed the organic character of the historical process of development. The continuity of this development binds the present and future condition of a national civilization to its historical past. The distinction between living and dead elements in the historical tradition of a people was also exclusively oriented to biotic analogies in the process of cultural development.

But these analogies are of a retrospective character. They refer backward in the order of time to an earlier aspect of our experience which lacks a normative character.

Development in its biological sense is not ruled by norms, i. e., by rules relating to what *ought to be,* but by laws of nature. In the biotic aspect of time the development of a multi-cellular living organism displays only the natural phases of birth, ripening, adolescence, age and decline. But in the historical process of cultural development a normative human vocation reveals itself, a cultural task committed to man at his creation. This task cannot be fulfilled except in the anticipatory, or prospective direction of time in which the historico-cultural aspect or our temporal world opens up its sense by unfolding its anticipatory moments. You will remember that anticipatory moments in the structure of an experiential aspect are those analogical moments which refer forwards to aspects occupying a later place in the temporal order of our experience.

We have established that all the aspects which in this order are founded on the logical mode of experience, inclusive of the historical aspect, are of a normative character. Therefore, the nuclear moment of the historico-cultural mode of development, namely, formative power, has itself a normative sense, since it implies a normative cultural vocation and task, committed to man at creation. Even the most terrible misuse of cultural power in our sinful world cannot make power itself sinful, nor can it detract from the normative sense of man's cultural vocation.

Until the cultural historical aspect of a human society discloses the anticipatory moments of its meaning, it shows itself to be in a rigid and primitive condition. Primitive cultures are enclosed in undifferentiated organized communities, which display a strong tendency towards isolation. As long as such primitive societies maintain their isolation in history, there can be no question of cultural development in the sense in which it is understood in historiography proper.

They display a totalitarian character, since they include their members in all the spheres of their personal life, and the temporal existence of the individual is completely dependent on membership of the family or sib, respectively, and of the tribal community. There is no room as yet for a differentiation of culture in the particular spheres of formative power, those, namely, of science, fine arts, commerce and industry, of state and church, and so forth. Since such undifferentiated communities fulfill all the tasks for which, on a higher level of civilization, particular organizations are formed, there is only one single undifferentiated cultural sphere. A rigid tradition, often deified by a pagan belief, and anxiously guarded by the leaders of the group, has the monopoly of formative power. The development process by which such cultural communities are formed shows only analogies of the biotic phases of birth, ripening, adolescence, age and decline. The duration of their existence is dependent on that of the popular and tribal communities by which they are sustained. They may vanish from the scene without leaving any trace in the history of mankind. This is how radical historicism conceived the course of every civilization and thus Spengler predicted the inescapable decline of Western culture.

But the situation is quite different in the historical development of cultures that are opened up. From the ancient cultural centers of world-history, such as Babylon, Egypt, Palestine, Crete, Greece, Rome, Byzantium, essential tendencies of development passed over into medieval and modern Western civilization. They fertilized the Germanic and Arabian cultures and this fertilization has given rise to new forms of civilization. This opened-up cultural development has been freed from rigid dependence upon the living conditions of small popular or tribal communities. It does not move within the narrow boundaries of a closed and undifferentiated cultural group. But, like a fertilizing stream, it is always seeking new channels along which to continue its course.

The process by which the cultural aspect of a society is opened up always occurs in a conflict between the guardians of tradition and the propounders of new ideas. The formative power of tradition is enormous, for, in a concentrated form it embodies cultural treasures amassed in the course of centuries. Every generation is historically bound to former generations by its tradition. We are all dominated by it to a much higher degree than we realize. In a primitive closed civilization its power is nearly absolute. In an opened up culture, tradition is no longer unassailable, but it has the indispensable role of guarding that measure of continuity in cultural progress without which cultural life would be impossible.

In the struggle with the power of tradition the progressive ideas of so-called molders of history have themselves to be purged of their revolutionary subjectivity and adjusted to the norm of historical continuity. Even Jacob Burckhardt, that great disciple of Leopold von Ranke, although strongly affected by the historicistic relativism, held to the norm of continuity as a last guarantee against the decline of all civilization.

The opening-up process of cultural life is characterized by the destruction of the undifferentiated and exclusive power of primitive communities. It is a process of cultural differentiation which is balanced by an increasing cultural integration. It is effected by the bursting of the rigid walls of isolation which had enclosed the primitive cultural life. This is achieved by submitting the latter to fruitful contact with civilizations which already have burst the bonds of tradition and had been opened up to outside influences.

Since August Comte and Herbert Spencer the criterion of differentiation and integration has been accepted by many sociologists to distinguish more highly developed from primitive societies. The process of differentiation was viewed as a consequence of the division of labor, and an attempt was made to explain it in a natural scientific manner in analogy to the increasing differentiation of organic life in the higher developed organisms. But I do not understand the term "cultural differentiation" in this pseudo-natural scientific sense.

Much rather I have in mind a differentiation in the typical structures of the different social relationships presenting themselves in a human society. A primitive sib or clan displays mixed traits of an extended family, a business organization, a club or school, a state, a religious community, and so forth. In a differentiated society, on the other hand, all these communities are sharply distinguished from one another, so that each of them can reveal its proper inner nature, notwithstanding the fact that there are all kinds of interrelations between them. Each of these differentiated communities has its own typical historico-cultural sphere of formative power, whose inner boundaries are determined by the inner nature of the communities to which they belong.

The typical structures of these communities are really structures of individuality, since they are typical structures of an individual societal whole. With the exception of the natural communities such as marriage and family, which have a typical biotical foundation, they are all typically founded in historico-cultural power formations, which presuppose the process of cultural differentiation and integration. Consequently, although they cannot be realized before this historical process has started, their typical structures can no more be variable than the modal structures of their different aspects, since they determine the inner nature of the differentiated communities. As such, they must be founded in the order of creation, which has determined the inner nature of all that presents itself within our temporal world. And they are not to be traced in a natural scientific way, since they are structural norms, which may be violated by man.

In the temporal world-order norms are only given as principles which need a formation by man in accordance with the level of historical development of a society. The societal forms which they assume in this way, are consequently of a variable character; but the structural principles, to which these forms give a variable positive content, are not variable historical phenomena, since they alone make all variable formations of the societal communities possible. Neither the inner nature of marriage, nor that of the family, the state, the church, an industrial community, and the like, are variable in time, but only the social forms in which they are realized.

The Historical school stressed the absolute individuality of any national community. But it overlooked the typical structures of individuality which determine the inner nature of the different communities, inclusive of the national one, which as such cannot be of a merely historical character. Nevertheless, it is true that the process of cultural differentiation and integration is at the same time a process of increasing individualization of human cultural life; for it is only in an opened up and differentiated civilization that individuality assumes a really historical significance.

It is true that in primitive, closed cultural areas individuality is not altogether lacking. But in consequence of the rigid dominance of tradition this individuality retains a certain traditional uniformity, so that from generation to generation such closed cultures display in general the same, individual features. It is for this reason that historiography in its proper sense takes no interest in these cultural individualities.

As soon, however, as the process of differentiation and integration commences, the historical task of individual cultural dispositions and talents becomes

manifest. Every individual contribution to the opening up of the cultural aspect of human society becomes in the course of time a contribution to the
cultural development of *mankind,* which has a world-
wide perspective. Accordingly, the individuality of
cultural leaders and groups assumes a deepened historical sense.

It is the opening-up process of human culture also
which alone can give rise to *national* communities.
A nation, viewed as a socio-cultural unit, should be
sharply distinguished from the primitive, ethnical
unit, which is called a popular or tribal community.
A real national cultural whole is not a natural product
of blood and soil, but the result of a process of
differentiation and integration in the cultural formation of human society. In a national community all
ethnical differences between the various groups of a
population are integrated into a new individual
whole, which lacks the undifferentiated totalitarian
traits of a closed and primitive ethnic unit as a tribe
or folkship. The different peoples of the United
States of America are doubtless united in a national
community, but how different are the ethnical components which are integrated into this national whole.

It was, therefore, an unmistakable proof of the
reactionary character of the myth of blood and soil
propagated by German Nazism that it tried to undermine the national consciousness of the Germanic
peoples by reviving the primitive ethnic idea of
Volkstum. Similarly, it is an unmistakable proof of
the retrograde tendency of all modern totalitarian

political systems that they attempt to annihilate the process of cultural differentiation and individualization by a methodical mental equalizing (*Gleichschaltung*) of all cultural spheres; for this equalizing implies a fundamental denial of the value of the individual personality in the unfolding (opening-up) process of history.

So we may posit that the norm of cultural differentiation, integration and individualization is really an objective norm of the historical unfolding process of human society. It is founded in the divine world-order, since it indicates the necessary conditions of this prospective unfolding process, without which mankind cannot fulfill its historical task committed to it by the great cultural commandment. Furthermore, it provides us with an objective criterion to distinguish truly progressive from reactionary tendencies in history.

The unfolding or opening-up process of the cultural-historical aspect occurs in the anticipatory or prospective direction of the temporal order; it must, therefore, be possible to indicate the anticipatory moments in its modal structure by which the inner coherence of meaning of the historical process of development with the subsequently arranged normative aspects of our temporal horizon of experience reveals itself. Historicism is not able to do so, since it has reduced these normative aspects to mere modalities of the historical process of development. Consequently, it denies their irreducible character and meaning.

To begin with, the progressive unfolding process of history is characterized by the disclosure of a symbolic, or linguistic anticipation in the historical mode of experience. The linguistic aspect of our experiential horizon is that of communication by medium of signs which have a symbolical meaning. These signs may be words or other symbols and they play an essential role in our social experience. In the opening-up process of historical development that which really has an historical significance begins to separate itself from what is historically insignificant. This gives rise to a symbolical signifying of historical facts in order to preserve the memory of them.

Hegel and von Ranke held that history proper did not start before the need arose to preserve the memory of historical events by means of chronicles, records and other means. The so-called *Kulturkreislehre* in ethnology, which seeks to trace genetic continuity in the cultural evolution of mankind from the so-called primeval cultures of pre-history to civilizations at the highest level of development of civilization, has denied that the presence of memorials can be of any essential importance for the delimitation of this historical field of research. As its founder, Frobenius, has said, "History is action, and in comparison with this, how unessential is its symbolical recording." The truth is, however, that the rise of such memorials is an unquestionable criterion of the cultural unfolding of a society in a progressive sense. Consequently, a depreciation of the rise of historical memorials with respect to their significance for the historical development of mankind, testifies to a lack of insight into the modal structure of the historical aspect of experience in its opening-up process. The fact that historical memorials, or at least, reliable oral historical informations are lacking in primitive society and that only mythological representations of the genesis and development of their cultural life are found, cannot be unessential. The relatively uniform course of their process of development has not yet given the Muse of history any material worth recording as memorable in a really historical sense. An as yet closed historical consciousness clings to the biotic analogies in cultural development and inclines to a mythological interpretation of its course under the influence of a primitive religion of organic life.

The disclosure of the symbolic or linguistic anticipation in the unfolding process of the historical aspect of experience is indissolubly linked to a disclosure of cultural intercourse between different nations, which are caught up in the stream of world history. Cultural intercourse between different nations in this international sense is an anticipatory moment in the process of historical development referring forwards to the opening up of the modal aspect of conventional social intercourse.

Since the process of cultural differentiation leads to an increasing typical diversity of cultural spheres, there is a constant danger that one of these spheres may try to expand its formative power in an excessive manner at the expense of the others. Indeed, since the dissolution of the ecclesiastically unified culture which prevailed in medieval European civilization, there has been a running battle between the emancipated cultural spheres of the state, of natural science, of industry and commerce, and so forth, to acquire the supremacy one over the other.

In the progressive unfolding process of history, therefore, the preservation of a harmonious relationship between the differentiated cultural spheres becomes a vital interest of the entire human society. But this cultural harmony can be guaranteed only if the process of historical development complies with the normative principle of cultural economy. This principle forbids any excessive expansion of the formative power of a particular cultural sphere at the expense of the others. Here the aesthetic and economic anticipations in the historical mode of experience reveal themselves in their unbreakable mutual coherence. Both principles, that of cultural economy and that of cultural harmony, appeal to the inner nature of the differentiated cultural spheres as determined by the typical structures of individuality of the spheres of society to which they belong. Thus they, too, are well founded in the divine world order. In the unfolding (opening-up) process of human culture, as soon as the natural bounds of the different cultural spheres are ignored through an excessive expansion of one of them, disastrous tensions and conflicts arise in human society. This may evoke convulsive reactions on the part of those cultural spheres which are threatened, or it may even lead to the complete ruin of a civilization, unless counter-tendencies in the process of development manifest themselves before it is too late and acquire sufficient cultural power to check the excessive expansion of power of a particular cultural factor.

It is in such consequences of the violation of the principles of cultural economy and harmony in the historical unfolding-process that the juridical anticipation in history comes to light. At this point we find ourselves confronted with the Hegelian adage: *"Die Weltgeschichte ist das Weltgericht."* I do not accept this dictum in the sense in which Hegel meant it; but rather in the sense that the violation of the normative principles to which the unfolding process of the cultural historical aspect of human society is subject is avenged in the course of world-history. This may be verified by observing the consequences of such violations.

When, finally, the question is asked concerning the deepest cause of disharmony in the unfolding process of history, we come face to face with the problem concerning the relationship between faith and culture and with the religious basic motives which operate in the central sphere of human life.

The disharmony in question belongs, alas, to the progressive line of cultural development, since it can only reveal itself in the historical unfolding process of cultural differentiation.

The conflicts and tensions which are particularly to be observed in modern Western civilization, cannot occur in a primitive, closed culture. Since any expansion of the formative power of mankind over the world gives rise to an increasing manifestation of human sin, the historical opening-up process is marked by blood and tears. It does not lead to an earthly paradise.

What, then, is the sense in all this extreme endeavor, conflict, and misery to which man submits in order to fulfill his cultural task in the world? Radical Historicism, as it manifested itself in all its consequences in Spengler's *Decline of the West,* deprived the history of mankind of any hope for the future and made it meaningless. This is the result of the absolutization of the historical aspect of experience; for we have seen that the latter can only reveal its sense in an unbreakable coherence with all the other aspects of our temporal experiential horizon. This temporal horizon itself refers to the human ego as to its central point of reference, both in its spiritual communion with all other human egos and in its central relationship to the Divine Author of all that has been created.

Ultimately, the problem of the meaning of history revolves around the question: "Who is man himself and what is his origin and his final destination?" Outside of the central biblical revelation of creation, the fall into sin and redemption through Jesus Christ, no real answer is to be found to this question. The conflicts and dialectical tensions which occur in the process of the opening-up process of human cultural life result from the absolutization of what is relative. And every absolutization takes its origin from the spirit of apostasy, from the spirit of the *civitas terrena,* the kingdom of darkness, as Augustine called it.

There would be no future hope for mankind and

for the whole process of man's cultural development if Jesus Christ had not become the spiritual center and his kingdom the ultimate end of world-history.

This center and end of world-history is bound neither to the Western nor to any other civilization. But it will lead the new mankind as a whole to its true destination, since it has conquered the world by the divine love revealed in its *self-sacrifice*.

Philosophy and Theology—I

It may seem a dangerous enterprise for a non-theologian to speak concerning the relation between philosophy and theology. Nevertheless, as representative of a philosophical trend which claims to have a radical Christian starting-point, I have been obliged to do so; especially since I am of the opinion that this Christian philosophy does not derive its fundamentals from theology in its scientific sense, and, therefore, should be sharply distinguished from the latter.

It is not surprising that many theologians are nonplussed by this point of view. And this initial doubt may easily change into suspicion when this new philosophy subjects the traditional philosophical fundamentals of dogmatic theological thought to a radical criticism and requires an inner reformation of these fundamentals from the biblical viewpoint.

Such suspicion is understandable, since philosophy has been a dangerous rival to Christian theology from the very outset. Ever since the Greek thinker, Parmenides, the founder of Western metaphysics, philosophical theory has been opposed to popular belief. It presented itself as the pathway of truth over against that of *doxa* (deceitful opinion), bound by sensory representations and emotions. In Plato's famous dialogue, *Phaedo,* Socrates says that it is only destined to the philosophers to approach to the race of the gods. It was the common conviction of all Greek thinkers, who held to the possibility of theological knowledge, that true theology can only be of philosophical character and cannot be founded on faith, but on theoretic thought only. It is true that Plato did not reject the possibility of a divine revelation, received in a state of holy enthusiasm. But he denied that such revelations could be in any sense the source of real theological knowledge.

It is, therefore, completely understandable that the Church Fathers in their treatises on Christian doctrine emphasized that Christian theology has its own principle of knowledge, namely, the Word-revelation. And, because it possesses this principle, which contains the absolute truth, Christian theology surpasses, in their opinion, all pagan philosophy in its certainty of knowledge. Theoretic thought cannot achieve truth, except it be enlightened by this principle. Therefore, pagan philosophy is full of errors and cannot be accepted as an autonomous science. Christian theology is itself the supreme science, it is the true Christian philosophy. Greek and Graeco-Roman philosophy, at their very best, can render some services to the *sacra doctrina,* provided, however, that they remain servants, subject to the control of theology.

It was especially Augustine who defended this view of the relation between philosophy and Christian theology. His rejection of the autonomy of philosophical thought is quite in accordance with the position of the new Christian philosophy which I had in mind at the outset of this lecture. But his view of the relation between Christian theology and philosophy suffers from an ambiguous use of the term theology. On the one hand, this word is used in the sense of the true knowledge of God and ourselves, and it refers to the holy doctrine of the Church. As such it cannot have a theoretical, scientific meaning, as will become evident presently. But on the other hand, Christian theology refers to a theoretical explanation of the articles of faith in their scientific confrontation with the texts of Holy Writ and with heretical views. In this sense, Christian theology is bound to theoretical human thought which cannot claim the infallibility of God's Word.

It was the influence of Greek philosophy which led to the fatal step of confusing theoretical Christian theology with the true knowledge of God and true self-knowledge (*Deum et animam scire*). The theological *gnosis*, permeated by Greek philosophical ideas, was elevated above the simple belief of the congregation. The whole conception of the so-called sacred theology as the *regina scientiarum* was of Greek origin. In the third book of his *Metaphysics*, chapter two, Aristotle says that the metaphysical doctrine of the ultimate goal and of the good, has the control and guidance over all other sciences, which, as its slaves, are not even allowed to contradict its truths. This statement clearly refers to the metaphysical knowledge of God, which in the second chapter of the first book was called the "guiding and most estimable science." Consequently philosophical theology was considered the Queen of all sciences.

This thesis of Aristotle was now applied to Christian theology in its theoretical, dogmatical sense. And this theology in turn was denominated as Christian philosophy. This meant that philosophical problems were merely discussed in a theological context.

In the 9th Century, John Scotus Erigena defended the thesis that true philosophy is identical with true religion. In his treatise on predestination he appealed to Augustine's treatise on true religion to corroborate this view. And in line with Augustine he identified Christian philosophy with dogmatical theology as the theoretical explanation of the canons of the Christian religion. "What else is true philosophy, than the explanation of the rules of true religion?"

This identification of dogmatical theology with Christian philosophy on the one hand, and, with the Christian religion as expressed in the holy doctrine of the Church, on the other, remained characteristic of the Augustinian tradition in Scholasticism.

The *Summa Theologiae* of Thomas Aquinas, which introduced a new view, displays the same fundamental ambiguity in the use of the terms, "theology" and *"sacra doctrina."* This prodigious work starts with a discussion of the question as to whether *sacra doctrina* is necessary *ad humanam salutem* and whether it is a science. These questions are answered in the affirmative.

It is necessary *ad humanam salutem* that there be a

doctrine according to the divine revelation in addition to the philosophical sciences, which are studied by the light of the natural human reason alone. And it is science of a higher rank than philosophy since its principle of knowledge is of a supra-natural character. As such it does not need the necessary aid of the philosophical sciences, though it can use them as its slaves to facilitate the understanding of its supra-natural truths. This is justified by the insufficiency of the human intellect which cannot understand the supra-natural truths of the holy doctrine without the basis of the natural truths which are known by reason alone.

These explanations have puzzled the commentators of the *Summa* not a little. What was meant by *"sacra doctrina"?* Thomas even identified it with Holy Scripture. *"Sacra Scriptura seu doctrina,"* so he wrote in his discussions on the scientific character of the holy doctrine.

Some commentators were of the opinion that by *sacra doctrina* the Christian faith was meant. Others interpreted it as theology in its proper, scientific sense. Again others ascribed to it the sense of the holy doctrine of the church viewed apart from theology and faith. Pope Leo XIII put an end to this uncertainty in his Encyclical *Aeterni Patris* in which he emphatically established that theology needs philosophy to give it the character and spirit of a science.

In any case, Thomas' view of the relation between Christian theology and philosophy differs in principle from that of Augustine. Thomas no longer identifies dogmatical theology and Christian philosophy. The question of a Christian philosophy no longer exists. Philosophy is accepted as an autonomous science including a philosophical or natural theology which refers to the natural light of reason alone. The Thomistic philosophy is the Aristotelian system at some points elaborated in an original way and mixed with Augustinian, Neo-platonic and Stoic ideas. Christian theology, on the other hand, is elevated to the rank of a supra-natural science surpassing philosophy both in dignity and in certainty of knowledge, due to its infallible, supra-natural principles originating in divine revelation. Since the natural truths of philosophy cannot contradict the supra-natural verities of holy Christian doctrine, the Aristotelian philosophy is accommodated to the latter, as far as appearances are concerned. Nevertheless, philosophy itself is withdrawn from the internal control of the Word of God. And the supra-natural character of Christian theology is justified by the fact that it must take its knowledge from divine revelation. But the very problem concerning the scientific character of this knowledge is masked by the ambiguous use of the term *sacra doctrina.* This led Thomas to a fatal identification of theology with the Holy Scriptures, on the one hand, and with the doctrine of the Church, on the other.

The lack of a sharp distinction between the Word revelation as the central principle of knowledge and the proper scientific object of dogmatic theology has maintained itself in the later discussions concerning the relation between dogmatic theology and philosophy, both in Roman Catholic and in Protestant circles. For the moment I shall restrict myself to the view developed by Karl Barth in the first volume of his *Kirchliche Dogmatik,* since it is representative of an influential trend in contemporary Reformed theology.

On the one hand, Barth opposes dogmatic theology to philosophy in a radical way. The former is instrumental to the true knowledge of God in Jesus Christ. The principle of theological knowledge is the Word of God, and this Word is a consuming fire for all philosophy. For the latter can only originate from autonomous human thought which is corrupted by sin. A Christian philosophy is a *contradictio in terminus.* This is why Barth, in sharp opposition to the view of Dr. Abraham Kuyper, even denies that the epistemology of theology is of a philosophical character. Dogmatic theology, as an instrument of God's Word, must elaborate its own epistemology without interference from philosophy.

On the other hand, Barth is obliged to admit that dogmatical theology, as a science, does not have another intellectual organ at its disposal than that of which philosophy also avails itself, namely, theoretical thought, which is thoroughly inadequate to true theological thought. This is the reason that the theologian cannot escape from philosophical notions. He may take them from all kinds of systems, provided that he does not bind himself to any one of them and employs these notions only in a purely formal sense by detaching them from their material philosophical contents.

Ignoring for the moment this very problematical distinction between a formal and a material use of philosophical concepts, we observe that Barth, too, employs the term "theology" in an ambiguous way. On the one hand, he understands by it the true knowledge of God in Jesus Christ; on the other, dogmatic science of the truths of the Christian faith revealed in the Holy Scriptures. But he does not distinguish these two meanings in a sufficient manner.

If we wish to succeed in positing the problem concerning a Christian philosophy and its relation to dogmatic theology in a clear way, we must in the first place avoid any ambiguity in the use of the terms and define what we understand by them.

We wish to establish at the outset that the true knowledge of God and of ourselves (*Deum et animam scire* in the Augustinian sense) surpasses all theoretical thought. This knowledge cannot be the theoretical object either of a dogmatical theology or of a Christian philosophy. It can only be acquired by the operation of God's Word and the Holy Spirit in the heart, that is to say, in the religious center and root of our entire human existence and experience. True knowledge of God and self-knowledge are the central presuppositions both of a biblical theology (in its scientific, theoretical sense) and, of a Christian philosophy insofar as the latter has a really biblical starting-point. This implies that the central principle of knowledge of dogmatic theology and that of Christian philosophy ought to be the same.

From the radical and integral biblical standpoint it

is impossible to accept the scholastic Thomistic distinction between a natural sphere of knowledge wherein the natural light of reason is sufficient, and a supra-natural sphere, wherein our knowledge is dependent on the divine Word-revelation. This distinction testifies to a lack of real self-knowledge, caused by a departure from the biblical viewpoint. Theoretical thought is not an independent substance, as Aristotle supposed. It is always related to the I, the human self; and this ego, as the center and radical unity of our whole existence and experience, is of a religious nature. Therefore real self-knowledge is dependent on the knowledge of God, since the ego is the central seat of the *imago Dei.*

Without true self-knowledge it is impossible to acquire an insight into the real relation between dogmatic theology and philosophy. For both, theological and philosophical thought, have their center in the same human ego. This I is the central reference point of the whole temporal order of our experience. *I* experience, and not an abstract sensory or intellectual function of my consciousness. Within the horizon and order of time, however, our experience displays a great diversity of fundamental aspects or experiential modes, which, as such, do not refer to a concrete *what,* i. e., to concrete things or events of our empirical world, but only to the *how,* i.e., a special *manner* of experiencing them.

In order to avoid the multivocality of the term "aspect" in common speech, I shall call these fundamental modes of our temporal experience, its *modal* aspects. A brief enumeration may suffice, for the present, to get a general view of the modal diversity of our experience within the order of time.

Within this temporal order our experience displays a numerical aspect, a spatial aspect, an aspect of extensive movement, an aspect of energy in which we experience the physico-chemical mode of change, a biotic aspect or that of organic life, a sensitive aspect or that of feeling and sensory perception, a logical aspect, *i. e.*, the analytical mode of distinction in our experience lying at the foundation of our logical concepts and judgments. Further, our temporal horizon of experience displays an historical aspect, or, that of the cultural mode of development of social life, an aspect of symbolical signification lying at the foundation of all linguistic phenomena; and finally an aspect of social intercourse, an economic, an aesthetical, a juridical, a moral and a faith aspect.

All these fundamental and irreducible modalities of our experience have their common foundation in the order of time, established by the creative will of God. This order of time has arranged them in an irreversible succession and keeps them in an unbreakable mutual coherence. This is why the modal aspects of our experience are essentially modes of time, which in each of these expresses itself in a specific modal sense. Beyond the temporal horizon of our experience this diversity of modal aspects loses its sense and foundation. Neither the human I, as the religious center and radical unity of human existence, nor

God, whose image, according to the order of creation, finds its central expression in the human ego, are to be found within this modal diversity of our temporal horizon.

In the human ego, as the central seat of the *imago Dei,* God had concentrated the entire meaning of the temporal world into a radical religious unity. Man, created in the image of God, should direct all the temporal functions and powers of his existence and those of his whole temporal world unto the service of God. This he was to accomplish in the central unity of his ego by loving God above all. And because, in the order of creation, every human ego in this central religious sense was united with every other human ego in a central communion of the service of God, the love for the neighbor was included in the love of God. We cannot love God without loving His image, expressed in the ego of ourselves and that of our fellow-men. Therefore, the entire divine Law for God's creation displays its radical unity in the central commandment of love, addressed to the heart, i. e., religious center of human life.

We cannot understand the radical and central sense of this commandment as long as we relate it only to the moral aspect of our temporal existence. Just as in the human ego *all* the aspects of our temporal experience and existence find their central reference point, so the commandment of love is the central unity of all God's different ordinances for the temporal world. For, it is not only the individual temporal existence of man which is centered in a radical unity. Much rather it is our whole temporal world, the "earth" as it is called in the initial words of the book of Genesis, which, according to the order of creation, finds its center in the religious root of mankind, i. e., in the spiritual community of the hearts of men in their central communion with God, the Creator.

This is the radical and integral sense of creation, according to the Word of God. It is at the same time the self-revelation of God as Creator and the revelation of man to himself as being created in God's image. It reveals to us that even in his central position with respect to the temporal world, man is nothing in himself but that the fullness of meaning of his existence was only to reflect the divine image of his Creator.

This also determines the radical and central sense of the fall into sin. This apostasy concerns the root, the religious center of human existence. The spiritual life of man depended upon his listening to the Word of God with all his heart. As soon as man closed his heart and turned away from the Word of God by giving ear to the false illusion of being something in himself, i. e., of being like God, the *imago Dei* was radically darkened in him and he fell a prey to spiritual death.

This apostasy implied the apostasy of the whole temporal world which was concentrated in man's ego. Therefore the earth was cursed, because it had no religious root of its own, but was related to the religious root or center of human existence.

For the same reason the redemption by Jesus Christ

and the communion of the Holy Spirit, which makes us into members of His body, has a central and radical sense. In Christ mankind and the whole temporal world have received a new religious root in which the *imago Dei* is revealed in the fullness of its meaning.

Thus the central theme of the Holy Scriptures, namely, that of creation, fall into sin, and redemption by Jesus Christ in the communion of the Holy Spirit, has a radical unity of meaning, which is related to the central unity of our human existence. It effects the true knowledge of God and ourselves, if our heart is really opened by the Holy Spirit so that it finds itself in the grip of God's Word and has become the prisoner of Jesus Christ. So long as this central meaning of the Word-revelation is at issue we are beyond the scientific problems both of theology and philosophy. Its acceptance or rejection is a matter of life or death to us, and not a question of theoretical reflection. In this sense the central motive of the Holy Scripture is the common supra-scientific starting point of a really biblical theology and of a really Christian philosophy. It is the key of knowledge of which Jesus spoke in his discussion with the Scribes and lawyers. It is the religious presupposition of any theoretical thought, which may rightly claim a biblical foundation. But, as such, it can never become the theoretical object of theology; no more than God and the human I can become such an object.

Both theological and philosophical theoretical thought move within the boundaries of the temporal order of our experience with its diversity of modal aspects. Within this temporal order the central and radical unity of the meaning of creation is as it were refracted into a rich diversity of modalities, just as sunlight is refracted by a prism into a rich diversity of colors.

The different modal aspects of our temporal horizon of experience which we have briefly enumerated, determine in principle the different viewpoints under which empirical reality is considered and investigated by the special sciences. This analytical dissociation of our experience in its different modal aspects, which in the pre-scientific experiential attitude is in principle lacking, is characteristic of the theoretical attitude of thought. The theoretical attitude arises as soon as we begin to oppose the logical aspect of our thought to the non-logical modes of experience in order to gain a theoretical logical insight into the latter by dissociating the elements of their modal structure in an analytical way.

But these non-logical aspects offer resistance to the attempt at conceiving them in a logical manner, as the theoretical objects of our logical thought. This theoretical resistance of the object gives rise to fundamental theoretical problems of the different special sciences.

The mathematical sciences, for instance, give rise to the fundamental problems: What is number? What is space? What is extensive movement? Physics and chemistry give rise to the problem: What is energy? Biology gives rise to the problem: What is organic life? Jurisprudence implies the problem: What is the juridical mode of experience? And thus one could continue.

But none of these fundamental theoretical problems can be solved by these special sciences taken by themselves. They are in principle of a philosophical character. The reason is that the special sciences do not reflect on their special viewpoint as such. They concentrate entirely upon the variable, actual phenomena which present themselves within the experiential aspects relating to their fields of study, at least insofar as these sciences are not of a purely mathematical character. In other words, they do not make the modal aspects of our experience as such into their object of research, but only the real phenomena so far as they function in that special aspect which delimits their field of investigation. Real phenomena, however, such as concrete things, events, human acts, or communal and interpersonal relationships between men in a certain society, function in principle in all of the modal aspects of our experience. Plants and animals, for instance, present, as real perishable beings, not only a biotic aspect. They function equally in the numerical aspect, the spatial aspect, the physico-chemical aspect of energy-effect, the sensitive aspect of feeling and sensory perception, etc. They present themselves to our pre-scientific experience in the typical structure of an individual whole. This whole functions in the unbreakable coherence of all the modal aspects of our experience; nevertheless it is typically qualified by one of these aspects. Water, for instance, in case of adequate temperature conditions presents itself to our experience as a colorless liquid matter, qualified by its physico-chemical properties. Nevertheless, it functions also in the biotic aspect or that of organic life, as a necessary means to life; it functions equally in our sensory aspect of perception, in the cultural aspect, in the economic and the juridical aspects, etc., and even in the aspect of faith. Remember, for instance, what is said in the Bible about God's dominion over the waters, which can only be experienced by faith.

When a biologist considers water, he is only concerned with its biotic aspect, i. e., its function in organic life. Nevertheless, he cannot investigate its biotical function without taking into account its physico-chemical properties. This gives rise to the fundamental theoretical problem: What is the mutual relation between the physico-chemical and the biotic aspect of the typical total-structure of a living organism? A living organism, as a real individual whole, is doubtless qualified by its biotic aspect; nevertheless, it presents equally all the other aspects of our experiential world. But this fundamental problem concerning the mutual relation between the different modal aspects of an individual whole exceeds the boundaries of the special sciences. It is of a philosophical nature.

Let us consider another example which is of direct concern for theological science. When the theologian directs his theoretical attention to the church as an institutional organized community in our temporal world, he is confronted with a real societal whole; this whole is doubtless qualified by its faith-aspect as an institutional congregation of believers in Jesus

Christ. As such the church points beyond our temporal horizon to the central religious community between Christ and the members of his body of which it should be a temporal expression. But the organized institution is not identical with this so-called invisible church. It functions as a societal whole in all the modal aspects of our temporal experiential horizon. Thus the theologian is confronted with the unbreakable coherence of the faith-aspect of this church-institution with its other aspects, wherein it functions as a moral, a juridical, an economic, a linguistic, an historical, a psychological, a biotic, a spatial community, etc. What is the relation between these different aspects of the church-institution and how does this temporal communal whole relate to other communities such as the state, the family, the school, industrial organizations, trade unions, etc.?

These fundamental theoretical problems exceed the boundaries of all special sciences. They are of a philosophical character, since their solution requires a theoretical total view of our temporal horizon of experience. Can Christian dogmatic theology as such provide us with this philosophical total view? If so, then it cannot be a special science, but must — in line with the Augustinian conception — be considered to be identical wth Christian philosophy.

But this solution of the age-old problem concerning the relation between theology and philosophy is unacceptable both from the philosophical and from the theological point of view. It is true that theology in its scientific activity comes again and again in contact with other sciences, such as philology, jurisprudence, ethics, historiography, archaeology, logic, psychology, the natural sciences, etc. But this is also the case with the other special sciences. It certainly does not imply that theology as such would be philosophy. The latter has the indispensable task of giving us an insight into the inner nature and structure of the different modal aspects of our temporal horizon of experience and to give us a theoretical view of their mutual relation and inner coherence.

But theology can no more give us such a theoretical total-view than biology can. Therefore, the Thomistic distinction between philosophy and dogmatic theology, as such, constituted progress when compared with the Augustinian view which identified this theology with Christian philosophy. From the philosophical viewpoint this identification was equally unacceptable since it implies a misunderstanding of the real nature of the philosophical problems.

The criterion, however, which Thomas Aquinas used to delimit the field of philosophy from that of dogmatic theology, was unserviceable in a scientific sense, and must be entirely rejected from the central biblical point of view. From the scientific viewpoint, it furnished no single insight into the true theoretical object of theology and of philosophy. Instead, it introduced the false distinction between an autonomous natural sphere of knowledge having no other source than the natural light of theoretical thought, and a supra-natural sphere dependent on divine revelation and on the supra-natural gift of faith. In this way philosophy was abandoned to the influence of central religious motives, which have been unmasked by the Word of God as motives originating from the spirit of apostasy and idolatry.

As soon as we, on the basis of the central biblical standpoint, arrive with Augustine at the insight that philosophical thought cannot be self-sufficient, since it is always dependent on a religious starting-point, the entire Thomistic criterion for the distinction between philosophy and theology breaks down. Nevertheless, its influence on Reformed theology has been so strong, that even Dr. Kuyper in his *Encyclopaedie der Heilige Godgeleerdheid,* was unable to extricate himself from it, although he himself contradicted the Thomistic interpretation by calling his Encyclopedia a Christian philosophy.

It is impossible to acquire a clear insight into the relation between philosophy and theology from the biblical standpoint, before we have arrived at a clear delimitation of the special scientific viewpoint of dogmatic theology. For it is exactly to dogmatic theology that both the Augustinian and the Thomistic tradition ascribe the exclusive right to be qualified as a Christian science.

What is the proper scientific object of this theology? We shall try to find a satisfactory answer to this critical question in our second lecture.

Philosophy and Theology—II

We concluded our first lecture by asking the question: What is the proper scientific viewpoint of dogmatic theology? What is its proper theoretical object?

We have seen that this question cannot be answered by referring to the revelation of God in his Word as the only true source of theological knowledge. For, as the central principle of knowledge, this Word-revelation must become the foundation of the whole of Christian life, both in its practical and its scientific activity. In this central sense it cannot be the theoretical object of any science, but functions only as its central starting-point, or religious basic motive.

To find a satisfactory answer to the question at issue, we should consider that, as a science, dogmatic theology is bound to the theoretical attitude of thought. In our first lecture we have established that this theoretical attitude arises as soon as we begin to oppose the logical aspect of our thought to the *non-logical* aspects of our experience. This is necessary to gain a logico-theoretical insight into them, or, as in the case of the special sciences, into a special aspect of the real facts presenting themselves within the various modes of experience. Through this opposition of our logical thought-function to the non-logical aspect of our experience which delimits our scientific field of research, the latter becomes the scientific object of our thought. Because of the resistance which this object offers to our attempt to gain a systematic logico-theoretical insight into it, it gives rise to theoretical problems.

Now it has appeared that theology cannot give us a philosophical total view of the mutual relation and coherence between the different aspects of our experience within the temporal order. Consequently, it must be a special science. In other words, the proper scientific object of dogmatic theology can only be delimited through a special modal aspect of our temporal horizon of experience. As such it must be capable of being opposed to the logical aspect of our thought as a field of theoretical problems. Nevertheless, we can only gain theoretical insight into this field by joining our logical thought-function with that special aspect of our temporal experience which delimits our scientific theological viewpoint. This modal experiential aspect that delimits the specific theological point of view can be no other than the aspect of faith.

I am well aware that this thesis may raise a complex of misunderstandings. Those who hold to the traditional confusion of the central principle of theological knowledge with the scientific object of dogmatic theological thought will doubtless make the following objections: By speaking of faith in the sense of a special aspect of our temporal horizon of experience which delimits the particular scientific viewpoint of theology, you give evidence of a fundamental disregard for the supra-natural character of the Christian faith. This latter can never originate from human experience but is exclusively the result of the operation of the Holy Spirit in the preaching of God's Word. In addition, dogmatic theology can have no other object than the divine Word-revelation, which contains the complete doctrine of the Church. Holy Scripture cannot be understood without exegesis of its texts. This exegesis requires theological knowledge of the original texts. Consequently, Thomas Aquinas was not wrong when he said that a theological science of the divine revelation is necessary *ad humanam salutem*. We do not understand your distinction between the central basic motive of the Holy Scripture which would be of a supra-theological character, and the theoretical object of dogmatic theology as a science, which would be delimited by the faith-aspect of our temporal horizon of experience. How can you say that the divine revelation of creation, fall into sin, and redemption by Jesus Christ in the communion of the Holy Spirit, is withdrawn from the scientific field of research in dogmatic theology? These subjects have always been the very basic materials of any theological dogmatics. Withdrawing them from the latter would amount to a complete destruction of theology.

What shall be our answer to these serious objections? I am sorry if my explanation concerning the scientific field of research of dogmatic theology seems not clear at first sight. The difficulties and questions to which it gives rise do not concern the divine Word-revelation, but exclusively the scientific character and bounds of a theological dogmatics and exegesis. And it is necessary *ad humanam salutem* to go into these difficulties in a serious way. For dogmatic theology is a very dangerous science. Its elevation to a necessary mediator between God's Word and the believer amounts to idolatry and testifies to a fundamental misconception concerning its real character and position. If our salvation be dependent on theological dogmatics and exegesis, we are lost. For both of them are a human work, liable to all kinds of error, disagreement in opinion, and heresy. We can even say that all heresies are of a theological origin. Therefore, the traditional confusion between God's Word as the central principle of knowledge and the scientific object of theological dogmatics and exegesis must be wrong in its fundamentals. For it is this very confusion which has given rise to the false identification of dogmatic theology with the doctrine of Holy Scripture, and to the false conception of theology as the necessary mediator between God's Word and the believers.

The theoretical object of scientific thought can never be the full or integral reality. The reason is that the object of theoretical thought, as such, can only result from a theoretical abstraction. It originates from the theoretical dissociation of the different aspects of experience and empirical reality, which in the temporal order of the divine creation are only given in an unbreakable continuous coherence. As soon as we oppose a non-logical aspect of our experience to the theoretical logical function of our thought, in order to make it into a theoretical problem this aspect becomes the scientific object of our thought. And even if our theoretical attention is not directed upon this aspect as such, but only upon the concrete facts presenting themselves within this aspect, the latter are never our theoretical object *in their full reality,* but only under the abstract scientific viewpoint which delimits our field of research.

As to theology this means that the divine Word-revelation can never become the theoretical object of theological research in the full reality wherein it presents itself to us. In its central religious sense it addresses itself to the heart, to the religious center of our existence, as a divine spiritual power, and not as an object of theological reflection. Therefore, the basic theme of Holy Scripture, namely that of creation, fall into sin and redemption by Jesus Christ in the communion of the Holy Spirit, can never become the scientific object of theology, in this central religious sense. As such it is much rather the supra-theological starting-point of all really biblical Christian thought, the key to the knowledge of God and of ourselves. But within the temporal order of our experience this Word-revelation manifests itself in the same modal diversity of aspects, which we find in our own temporal human existence. God's Word has entered our temporal horizon, just as it has become flesh in Jesus Christ, our Saviour. And it is only within the temporal diversity of experiential aspects that the divine revelation can become an object of **theological thought.**

It cannot be doubted that the temporal order of our experience, according to the divine order of creation, has a limiting aspect of faith, which in this sense is a fundamental mode of experience, clearly distinct from all other modes. The modal structure of this aspect, which determines its irreducible meaning, belongs to the order of creation, and could, as such, not be affected by sin. Sin cannot destroy anything of God's creation, it can only give to it a false, apostatic *direction*. Both, genuine Christian faith and apostatic faith, and even unbelief, can only function within the same modal aspect of faith which is inherent in the created temporal order of our experience. They all have a fundamental faith character, just as both the legal and illegal manner of behavior are of a juridical character and both a logical and an illogical manner of reasoning can only occur within the logical aspect of thought.

But the modal faith-aspect may not be identified with the real act of believing which in its full reality comes out of the heart, and, though *qualified* by its faith-aspect, presents also other aspects in the temporal order of experience. It is beyond discussion that the actual Chritian faith in its true sense can only originate from the operation of God's Word, as a central spiritual power, in the heart, i. e., the religious center of our existence. But this does not detract from the fact that it functions within the modal faith-aspect of our temporal experience which belongs to the temporal order of creation.

Now it should be considered that this aspect occupies an entirely exceptional place in this order; it is the limiting aspect that even in the kernel of its modal sense refers beyond the temporal order to the religious center of our existence and to the divine Origin of all that has been created. This modal kernel of the faith-aspect may be circumscribed as *that ultimate mode of certitude within the temporal order of experience which refers to an indubitable revelation of God touching us in the religious center of our existence.*

Now the living God has revealed himself in the whole of his creation, in all the works of his hands. But this revelation, which in the temporal order displays a rich diversity of aspects, finds its center of operation in the heart, the center and root of human existence, wherein God has expressed the central meaning of his image. And it is the faith-aspect in its modal meaning by means of which the divine revelation within the temporal order of our experience is related to this religious center of our consciousness and existence.

We should, however, consider that from the very beginning this revelation of God in all the works of his hands was not accessible to a would-be autonomous human understanding. This *phanerosis*, as it is called in the first chapter of the Epistle to the Romans, was elucidated and interpreted by the Word of God that addressed itself to the heart of man by mediation of the temporal function of faith. So long as the human heart was open to the Word of God, man was capable of understanding the sense of God's general *phanerosis* by means of his innate function of

faith. But as soon as this heart closed itself and turned away from the Word of God, as a result of its
apostasy, the faith-aspect of the temporal human experience was also closed. It was no longer the window
of our temporal experience, open to the light of
eternity, but it became the instrument of the spirit of
apostasy. Likewise the innate religious impulsion of
the human heart to transcend itself in order to find
rest in its divine origin, began to unfold itself in an
idolatrous direction. It is exclusively by the operation
of the Holy Spirit which regenerates the heart, that
the faith-aspect of our temporal experience can be re-
opened to the Word of God, so that its negative
direction is changed into a positive one. Thus it is
completely true that the living Christian faith can in
no way originate from the temporal experience of
man, who because of his apostasy is fallen prey to
spiritual death.

Nevertheless, its modal structure and general faith-
character belong to the temporal order of human experience as it is founded in the divine creation. Consequently, even Christian faith does not result from a
completely new creative act of God, as Barth thinks.
Therefore the scholastic Roman Catholic view of faith
as a supra-natural gift of God to the human intellect,
manifesting itself beyond the natural order of creation, should also be rejected from the biblical standpoint. It is only under the influence of the dualistic
religious motive of nature and grace that scholastic
theology has introduced this conception. But this
motive which has continued to rule both Roman
Catholic theology and Protestant scholasticism, is of

an unbiblical origin. It is a dialectical basic motive aiming at an accommodation of the central motive of Holy Scripture to religious motives of an apostate character, either to that of Greek philosophy or to that of modern Humanism.

This dualistic basic motive has deprived scholastic theology of the insight into the radical and integral character of the Word-revelation. It has led to a theological conception of human nature which has no room for the heart as the religious center and radical unity of human existence. By ascribing to the so-called natural reason an autonomy over against faith and the divine revelation, traditional scholastic theology merely gave expression to the false Greek view of reason as the center of human nature. Within the framework of the Roman Catholic ecclesiastic doctrine this caused no inner difficulties, since this doctrine did not accept the radical character of the fall into sin.

In Reformed theology, on the contrary, this unbiblical view of human nature could not fail to cause an inner contradiction with the biblical doctrine of sin and redemption. For, if human nature does not have a religious center or radix, how can the fall be of a radical character, i. e., touch the root of our nature? Sin cannot originate from man's intellect. If the latter would be the center of our human nature, independent from our central religious life, it would not be affected by sin. Therefore, Roman Catholic doctrine was consistent when it denied the inner corruption of human nature. And it is this very view of human nature which caused the problem of the relation between theology and philosophy to be posed on a fundamentally erroneous basis. The whole distinction between a so-called sacred theology and the so-called profane sciences issued from the unbiblical dualism inherent in the scholastic basic motive of nature and supra-natural grace.

It is a gladdening symptom of a re-awakening biblical consciousness, that under the influence of Augustinianism an increasing number of Roman Catholic thinkers, belonging to the movement of the so-called *nouvelle théologie,* have begun to oppose this dualistic view. They agree with the Reformed philosophical movement in the Netherlands in advocating the necessity of a Christian philosophy. On the other hand, we must observe that the Barthian view of theology as the exclusive Christian science and of its negative relation to philosophy, is still entirely penetrated by this dualism. This is a baffling fact, since, in sharp opposition to Roman Catholicism, Barth claims for his theology a radical biblical character. How is this to be explained? The reason is that Barth, though sharply opposing the synthetical Thomistic view of nature and grace, did not abandon this dualistic theme as such, which in the Augustinian view was still unknown. He merely replaced its synthetical conception, according to which nature is the autonomous basis of the supra-natural sphere of grace, by an antithetical one which denies any point of contact between the corrupted autonomous nature and the divine work of grace. Thus philosophy was excommunicated as such, because by nature it would be an autonomous product of natural thought which is corrupted by sin. Among all sciences only dogmatic theology was supposed to be capable of being permeated by the Word-revelation. In my opinion, this dualistic view betrays the after effects of the Occamistic Nominalism, which has especially influenced the Lutheran view concerning the impossibility of a Christian philosophy.

However, if the possibility of a Christian philosophy is denied, one should also deny the possibility of a Christian theology in the sense of a science of the biblical doctrine. Barth, however, emphatically maintains this scientific character of theology, though, in complete accordance with Thomas Aquinas, he places all stress on its supra-natural principle of knowledge. But he admits that this theology is obliged to avail itself of the same theoretical thought as philosophy does. How then can this theological thought claim a Christian character? Luther called natural reason a harlot which is blind, deaf, and dumb with respect to the truths revealed in the Word of God. But, if this prostitute can become a saint by its subjection to the Word of God, it is hardly to be understood why this wonder would only occur within the sphere of theological dogmatics. Why may not philosophical thought as well be ruled by the central motive of Holy Scripture? It is certainly not the biblical basic motive in its radical and integral sense which led many theologians to the conclusion that philosophy has nothing to do with the Kingdom of God. It is only the non-biblical dualistic motive of nature and grace that led them astray and that inspired Barth's view that man may expect that, at least in general, God has bound the operation of his Word to a "theological space" in which the Bible, ecclesiastical preaching, and theology, as to their instrumental function, are placed on the same level. It is this scholastic basic-motive which has also impeded the necessary transcendental critique of theological thought, both as to its scientific object and as to its starting point.

We have remarked that the object of dogmatic theological thought can only be found within the temporal order of experience. We have established that it can be nothing but the Divine Word-revelation as it presents itself within the modal aspect of faith. This latter is made into a theological problem in the theoretical attitude of thought by being placed over against the logical function of theological thinking. We must now try to realize the significance of the distinction between the Word of God in its full and actual reality and in its restricted sense as the object of theological thought. This is necessary in order to answer the question as to whether it is true that this distinction would withdraw from theological dogmatics its chief subject-matter, which would amount to a complete destruction of dogmatic theology in its traditional sense.

Let us first consider how the Word of God presents itself to us in its full and actual reality. The divine Word-revelation has entered our temporal horizon. The Word was made flesh and dwelt among us. This was the *skandalon* which was equally raised by the incarnation of the Word-revelation in the Holy Scriptures, a collection of books written by different men in the course of ages, be it through divine inspiration, yet related to all the modal aspects of our temporal horizon of experience. It is, however, only under the modal aspect of faith that we can experience that this Word-revelation in the Scriptures has been inspired by the Holy Spirit. And the actual belief through which we know with an ultimate certainty that it is so, cannot be realized in the heart, that religious center of our consciousness, except by the operation of the Word itself, as a spiritual power. What makes the diversity of books of the Old and New Testament into a radical spiritual unity? Their principle of unity can only be the central theme of creation, fall into sin, and redemption by Jesus Christ in the communion of the Holy Spirit, since it is the key to true knowledge of God and self-knowledge.

We have established that, in its central spiritual sense, as divine motive power addressing itself to our heart, this theme cannot become the theoretical object of theological thought, since it is the very starting point of the latter, insofar as theology is really biblical.

But dogmatic theology can doubtless engage in a theoretical reflection on creation, fall into sin, and redemption, insofar as their revelation is related to the faith aspect of our temporal experience, and forms the contents of articles of Christian belief. It is even possible that a theologian does so from a non-biblical starting point, such as the traditional scho-

lastic basic-motive of nature and grace. Starting from
this unbiblical motive, Thomas Aquinas considered
creation as a partly natural philosophical, partly
supra-natural truth. The fall was taken as merely the
loss of the supra-natural gift of grace, which did not
corrupt the rational nature of man, but only wounded
it. This theological view of creation and fall was
sanctioned as orthodox doctrine by the Roman
Catholic Church.

From this it may appear that there must be a
difference in principle between creation, fall and
redemption in their central sense as the key to knowledge, and in their sense as articles of faith, which may
be made into the object of theological thought. Insofar as Reformed theology, too, was influenced by
the scholastic basic motive of nature and grace, it
also developed dogmatic views which must be considered unbiblical. The Jewish Scribes and lawyers
had a perfect theological knowledge of the books of
the Old Testament. They wished, doubtless, to hold
to the creation, the fall and the promise of the coming Messiah as articles of the orthodox Jewish faith
which are also articles of the Christian faith. Nevertheless, Jesus said to them: "Woe unto you, for ye
have taken away the key of knowledge!"

This key of knowledge in its radical and integral
sense cannot be made into a theological problem. The
theologian can only direct his theological thought to
it as to its necessary supra-theoretical presupposition,
if he is really in the grip of it, and bear witness of its
radical meaning which transcends all theological

concepts. But when he does so, he is in no other position than the Christian philosopher, who accounts
for his biblical starting-point, or the simple believer,
who testifies to the radical sense of God's Word as the
central motive power of his life in Jesus Christ. In
other words, the true knowledge of God in Jesus
Christ and true self-knowledge are neither of a dog-
matic-theological, nor of a philosophical nature, but
have an absolutely central religious significance. This
knowledge is a question of spiritual life or death.
Even an orthodox theological dogmatics, however
splendidly elaborated, cannot guarantee this central
spiritual knowledge. Therefore, the scholastic term
sacra theologia testifies to an unbiblical over-estima-
tion of theology. All such theological problems as the
significance of the *imago Dei* before and after the
fall, the relation between creation and sin and that
of particular grace to common grace, that of the union
of the two natures in Jesus Christ, etc., can only arise
in the theoretical opposition of the faith-aspect to the
logical aspect of our thought. They are certainly
legitimate problems of theological dogmatics, but
exactly as theological problems they do not concern
the central basic motive of the Holy Scriptures as it
is operative in the religious center of our consciousness and existence. This spiritual basic motive is elevated above all theological controversies and is not in
need of theological exegesis, since its radical meaning
is exclusively explained by the Holy Spirit operating
in our opened hearts, in the communion of this Spirit.
This is the only really ecumenical basis of the Church
of Christ, which in its institutional temporal appear-

ance is hopelessly divided, and it is the ultimate divine judge both of all dogmatic theology and of all philosophy. This does not mean that this spiritual basic motive would be the basis of a Christendom above all dissensions of faith, as if it would have nothing to do with an ecclesiastical confession. On the contrary, it is the judge also of every ecclesiastical doctrine and will always remain the central basic principle of a continual reformation of the Church's doctrine. Every view which makes this central and radical sense of God's Word dependent on a theological dogmatics and exegesis, is unbiblical in its very fundamentals.

This radical biblical standpoint lies at the foundation of the reformed philosophy which during the last decennaries has been developed at the Free University of Amsterdam. It has inspired its radical critique of theoretical thought which applies both to philosophy itself and to theology. This critique, which is the key to an understanding of its philosophical intention and significance, has uncovered the inner point of connection between theoretical thought, in all of its manifestations, and the central religious basic motives which are its real, but often masked, starting-points. It has done so by showing from the inner structure and nature of theoretical thought itself its necessary presuppositions which are necessarily related to the central religious sphere of human consciousness. This means that the traditional dogma concerning the autonomy of theoretical reason as to the natural truths turns out to be untenable.

It is the central religious motive of theoretical

thought which, as its real starting-point, rules any philosophical view of the mutual relation and inner coherence between the different aspects of our temporal horizon of experience. This is why the biblical basic-motive cannot fail to bring about a salutary inner revolution in our entire philosophical view of temporal experience and of empirical reality. Neither philosophy, nor dogmatic theology, can be withdrawn from the radical and integral grip of this central basic-motive without their being abandoned to the influence of non-biblical motives.

However, Christian philosophy does not have the task and competence to go into the dogmatic and exegetical problems of theology except insofar as the philosophical and central religious fundamentals of theology as a theoretical science are at issue. For as soon as the fatal confusion between the central starting-point and the theoretical object of theology has been overcome, it must be evident that theology in its scientific sense is bound to philosophical fundamentals which are in turn dependent on the central religious motive of theoretical thought. The reason is that the faith-aspect of our temporal horizon of experience which delimits the theoretical object of theology *in its modal sense,* displays an intrinsic coherence with all the other experiential modes. This inner coherence between the different aspects finds expression in the modal structure of each of them, so that this structure reflects the integral temporal order of all the aspects in their established succession. This implies that the modal structure of the faith-aspect, just like that of all other experiential modes, displays an intricate character. On the one hand, it presents a central moment of its sense, which is its irreducible kernel. On the other, it displays a series of analogical moments, whose meaning is in itself multivocal and is only determined by the modal kernel of the faith-aspect. The analogical moments give expression to the inner coherence between this aspect and all the other modes of experience within the temporal order.

It is this analogical structure of the faith-aspect which obliges theology to avail itself of fundamental concepts of an analogical character. That is to say, these concepts are also used by the other special sciences, but in a different modal sense; nevertheless, there is an inner coherence between these different modal meanings. Such theological concepts of an analogical character are, for instance, that of time, number, space, movement, force and causality, life, emotion, distinction, power, symbol, signification and interpretation, justice, guilt, imputation and punishment, love, etc. It is of primordial concern that the theologian realizes the proper faith-sense of these analogical concepts in their theological use and does not confound this particular signification with that ascribed to them in other sciences. For such a confusion cannot fail to give rise to erroneous manners of posing theological problems. I refer, for example, to the question concerning the sense of the six days of creation. By disregarding the faith-aspect of the temporal order and by utilizing astronomical and geological concepts of time, theology was entangled in the following dilemma: if these days are not to be understood in the sense of astronomical days of twenty-four hours, they are to be interpreted as geological periods. A curious dilemma, indeed. For it has not occurred to any theologian to apply this alternative to the seventh day, the day on which God rested from all his work which he had made. This would be rightly considered blasphemy. But why was it overlooked that the same blasphemy presents itself if God's creative deeds are conceived in natural scientific time-concepts? The reason is that the theologians who posed the dilemma mentioned did not realize the fundamental difference between the divine creative deeds and the genetical process occurring within the created temporal order as a result of God's work of creation. Here the influence of Greek philosophy clearly manifested itself. For because of its pagan religious basic motive this philosophy excluded any idea of creation. It merely accepted a temporal genesis, at the utmost conceived of as the result of a formative activity of a divine mind which presupposes a given material. The scholastic accommodation of the biblical revelation of creation to this Greek idea of becoming gave rise to the false view that creation itself was a temporal process.

God's creative deeds surpass the temporal order because they are not subjected to it. But as a truth of faith God has revealed these creative deeds in the faith-aspect of this temporal order which points beyond itself to what is supra-temporal. It was God's will that the believing Jew should refer his six work days to the six divine creative works and the sabbath day to the eternal sabbathic rest of God, the Creator. This is the biblical exegesis given by the Decalogue. And it eliminates the scholastic dilemma concerning the exegesis of the six days of creation, which originated from a fundamental disregard of the faith-aspect of the temporal order. This disregard is also to be observed in the Augustinian interpretation of the six days as a literary form or framework of representation which lacks any temporal sense, though this conception is, no doubt, preferable by far to the astronomical or geological interpretation.

Theological pseudo-problems always arise when the analogical basic theological concepts are used in a non-theological sense. Remember, for instance, the Occamistic conception of God's omnipotence as an absolute power apart from God's justice, love, holiness, etc. In this way the analogical concept of power was conceived in the sense of a tyrannical arbitrariness, and certainly not in the sense of the Christian faith. Power in its original modal sense is the nuclear moment of the historico-cultural mode of experience; for culture is nothing but a controlling mode of formation, which exactly by its qualification as dominion over the material is fundamentally distinct from all modes of formation found in nature. But even in this original and nuclear modal sense power is only to be conceived in unbreakable coherence with the whole series of analogical experiential moments in the historico-cultural aspect in which the context with the other aspects finds expression. Similarly the analogy of power which we meet with in the modal structure of the faith-aspect cannot unfold its analogical meaning within this aspect apart from its unbreakable coherence with all the other analogies in this mode of experience. Any attempt to isolate such an analogy and to relate it in this isolation to God as a predicate of his self-revelation, amounts to an absolutizing of a temporal moment of our experience. It leads to the formation of idols which result in a meaningless nothingness. In the same way the theological meaning of the analogical concept of causality is misunderstood by conceiving predestination in a mechanical sense. The true theological meaning of all such analogical concepts can only reveal itself in the unbreakable coherence of the faith-aspect with all the other aspects of the temporal order of experience.

This is the reason why theology in its scientific sense needs a philosophical foundation. For it is philosophy alone which can provide us with a theoretical insight into the inner structure and the mutual coherence of the different aspects or modes of human experience. The only question is whether these philosophical fundamentals will be subject to the biblical religious basic motive, or to some non-biblical religious basic motive, originating from a complete or partial apostasy. It is only the radical and integral biblical starting-point which can free philosophy from prejudices implying a distortion of the structural order of the experiential aspects. The apostatical basic motives cannot fail to entangle philosophical **thought in absolutizing special aspects, whereby an** insight into their real structure and real coherence with the others is precluded in principle. It is a vain illusion to imagine that such philosophical views might be made harmless by accommodating them in an external way to the ecclesiastical doctrine to which the theologian holds.

By a perennial tradition, originating in the canonization of the Thomistic view, but already prepared by pre-Thomistic scholasticism, dogmatic theology has been bound to a scholastic philosophy, ruled by the unbiblical basic motive of nature and grace. In fact, it was an Aristotelian philosophy accommodated to the doctrine of the Church. The analogical character of the theological basic concepts was conceived from the viewpoint of the Aristotelian metaphysics, which started from the analogical concept of being, the so-called *analogia entis*. But this metaphysics, howsoever accommodated to the Church's doctrine, could not fail to turn away theological thought from the radical biblical standpoint, since its basic motive was incompatible with that of the Holy Scripture. I shall revert to this point in my next lecture.

By means of the metaphysical doctrine of the *analogia entis* dogmatic theology tried to account for the fact that Holy Scripture speaks about God in terms related to the modal diversity of our temporal order of experience. But this doctrine of the *analogia entis* had nothing to do with the Christian faith. Rather, it was supposed to be founded on natural reason alone in its pretended autonomy. Karl Barth rightly rejected this metaphysics of the *analogia entis*.

He called it an invention of the antichrist and replaced it by the *analogia fidei*, the analogy of faith.
But, as we have seen, it is exactly the analogical structure of faith which confronts theology with a basic
problem of philosophical character that cannot be
put aside.

If, as Barth thinks, Christian belief would really
have no single point of contact with human nature,
how can it display that analogical structure by which
it is bound even to the sensory aspect of our experience? How could we believe without having heard
the Word with the ear of sense, or without having
perceived the written words of the Bible with the eye
of sense, and having understood the lingual meaning
of the words? It is this very coherence of the faith-
aspect with all the other fundamental modes of temporal experience which is not explicable from the
theological viewpoint alone.

If the theologians deny the possibility of a bibli-
cally-founded philosophy, they are bound to take their
philosophical presuppositions from a so-called autonomous philosophy. It is a vain illusion to imagine
that the notions borrowed from such a philosophy
could be utilized by the theologian in a purely formal
sense. They imply a material content which is in-
solubly bound to the total theoretical view of experience and of reality. It has been pretended, for
instance, that the philosophical concept of substance
could be utilized by theology in a formal sense to
give expression to the essential unity of soul and body
in human nature. Nevertheless, this metaphysical con-

cept implied a Greek view of human nature excluding in principle the insight into the religious center of human existence. How could theology, on such a philosophical basis, do justice to the revelation of the creation in its radical biblical sense? How could it do justice to the pregnant biblical utterances concerning the heart as the inner center of human life? And the situation does not become better if theology turns away from the scholastic-Aristotelian philosophy in order to have recourse to modern philosophical views rooted in the basic motive of Humanism. In Europe there are many theologians who consider the contemporary humanist existentialism more biblical than Aristotelianism. I do not understand this opinion. The qualification "more biblical" is characteristic of the neo-scholastical attitude in theological and philosophical thought which only aims at an accommodation of this uprooted humanist existentialism to the biblical view without having realized the radical and integral character of the biblical basic motive. Genuine Humanistic basic views concerning man and his world of more or less biblical character do not exist. The biblical basic motive can only be accepted or rejected as a whole. And the same applies to the Humanist religious position.

Naturally this does not mean, that there are not to be found important elements of truth in humanist existentialism. But the philosophical total view from which they are interpreted does not allow of a partial acceptance from the biblical standpoint. It is an integral whole, ruled by the religious basic motive of Humanism.

Theology is above all in need of a radical critique of theoretical thought which, because of its biblical starting-point, is able to show the intrinsical influence of the religious basic motives both upon philosophy and theology. This is the first service which the new reformed philosophy can render its theological sister. In my next lecture I shall explain the necessity of this service a little more in detail.

Philosophy and Theology—III

In the last lecture I have shown why theology as a science of the dogmata of the Christian faith is in need of a philosophical foundation. The Christian life of faith as such, doubtless, does not need philosophy, nor does the divine Word-revelation need it. Neither of them is of a theoretical character. Dogmatical theology, on the contrary, is in its scientific character bound to the theoretical attitude of thought. It is continually confronted with the problem concerning the relation between its analogical basic concepts to those of the other sciences. This problem appeared to have an inner connection with the place which the faith aspect of our experience occupies in the temporal order of the experiential aspects. And this problem is of an intrinsically philosophical nature.

For theology the question is not, whether or not it should be philosophically founded. The only question is whether it is to seek its philosophical foundations in a Christian philosophy, ruled and reformed by the central biblical basic motive or if it should take them from the traditional scholastic or modern Humanist philosophy.

The influence of the scholastically-adapted Greek philosophy on dogmatic theology was the more dangerous, as the theologians, led astray by the traditional belief in the autonomy of natural reason, did not realize the anti-biblical presuppositions of this philosophy.

We should not forget that the process of decay of Reformation theology had begun since the restoration of this scholastic philosophy at the Protestant universities. This restoration effectuated by Melanchton and Beza, meant (unintentionally of course) a denial of the integral principle of the Reformation, which implied an inner reformation of the whole Christian life by its subjection to the radical and central authority of God's Word-revelation. It testified to the fact that the un-biblical religious basic motive of nature and grace had begun to regain an increasing influence on the theological and philosophical views of Protestantism. The Roman Catholic view in its Thomistic conception, according to which philosophy can have no other principle of knowledge than the natural light of reason, whereas theology has a supranatural source of knowledge in revelation, was completely taken over. But the return to this view implied a return to the scholastic foundation of dogmatic theology on the metaphysical fundamentals of the Aristotelian philosophy in its external accommodation to the doctrine of the Church. This meant that any attack upon the Aristotelian metaphysics was rightly felt as an attack upon the scholastic trend in Reformed theology itself. And inasfar as the influence of the Thomistic-Aristotelian metaphysics had even revealed itself in some formulations of the Reformed Confessions, especially in the Westminster Confession, this attack could be easily interpreted as a deviation from the Church's doctrine. But thereby an inescapable difficulty arose.

The Thomistic-Aristotelian view of human nature, which excluded the biblical revelation of the heart as the religious center of human life, was supposed to give expression both to a philosophical and to a theological truth. As a philosophical conception it was supposed to be provable by the natural light of reason alone; as a theological conception it sought support from different texts of Holy Scripture, which were supposed to corroborate it. This implied that a philosophical anthropology was ascribed to the Holy Scriptures; an anthropology, which was incompatible with the radical sense of the biblical revelation concerning creation, fall and redemption. But by so doing the only criterion at the disposal of Scholasticism for delimiting the field of research of theology from that of philosophy, appeared to fail. The only means to escape from effacing the bounds between them was to forbid the philosophers any independent consultation of the Holy Scriptures and to bind them to the Thomistic-Aristotelian view of human nature.

This solution of the difficulty was quite Roman Catholic, and it presupposed the Roman Catholic view of the infallible doctrinal authority of the Church. The Reformation, however, had rejected this authority in principle and had opened the Bible to all believers. In consequence, until the separation of church and state, there seemed to remain no other escape than that the church apply for help to the secular government in case of disagreement between philosophers and theologians about anthropological questions.

This road was followed in the Netherlands in the 17th century, when the contest between the adherents of the Cartesian philosophy and the theologians at the universities had led to serious troubles. The Cartesians defended the thesis that the material body and the rational soul are only accidentally united in human nature. The theologians held to the Thomistic-Aristotelian view of a substantial union between these two components. In the year 1656 the Estates of Holland and West-Friesland issued their famous resolution concerning the relation between philosophy and theology in consequence of a complaint lodged by the Synod of the Dutch Reformed Churches against the propagation of the Cartesian views with respect to subjects belonging to theology. This resolution began by applying the traditional scholastic criterion in order to delimit the bounds of philosophy and theology. Philosophy should restrict itself to questions which may be investigated by the natural light of reason alone; theology, on the other hand, should treat such subjects which are to be known only from the Word-revelation.

It was evident that a consistent application of this criterion could not fail to lead to the conclusion that the theological professors should abstain from teaching any philosophical theory of man. But this would have been unacceptable from the theological viewpoint, since the Thomistic-Aristotelian view of human nature was considered to be in accordance with the doctrine of Holy Scripture and thus was made into an article of faith. On the other hand the question at issue could not be withdrawn from philosophy and assigned to the exclusive competence of theology. For, both the scholastic philosophy, defended by the theologians, and the Cartesian philosophy, considered it as belonging to the essential problems of metaphysics. Consequently, the resolution of the Estates was obliged to take these difficulties into account. It established that theology has borrowed many terms, distinctions, and rules from other sciences, which in many respects can help to clarify the theological problems. On the other hand, it admitted that there are subjects which, though belonging also to the realm of faith, nevertheless may be examined and known by the natural light of reason alone. Therefore, the resolution recommended to the philosophers to treat such subjects less amply than the theologians who used arguments taken from the Holy Scriptures, the exegesis of texts, the refutation of older and contemporary heresies, etc.

Besides, according to the resolution, such matters can be understood much better and more securely from the Holy Scripture than from natural reason. Consequently, when the natural light of human reason would seem to lead us to other results, one should have more confidence in the divine authority alone

than in human reasoning. On these grounds the resolution prohibited a further propagation of the Cartesian theses which had given offense to the theologians. In this way the secular government tried to put
an end to the debate between the Cartesian philosophers and the theologians. But the resolution which
satisfied the wishes of the ecclesiastics, and followed, in
the main, the advice of the theological faculty of the
University of Leyden, showed at the same time to
what degree the spirit of Scholasticism had supplanted
the biblical spirit of the Reformation. The Thomistic
view of human nature as a composite of an immortal,
rational soul and a perishable material body united
as form and matter of one substance, had no more in
common with the biblical revelation about man than
the Cartesian conception. Both of them were metaphysical theories ruled by un-biblical religious basic
motives.

The whole idea that a philosophical knowledge of
human nature would be possible by the natural light
of human reason alone, i. e., independent of religious
presuppositions, testified to a fundamental apostasy
from the biblical starting-point. And the very fact that
scholastic theology sought to corroborate the Thomistic-Aristotelian view by texts of the Scripture showed
how much theological exegesis itself had come into
the grip of un-biblical basic motives.

Let us consider this situation a little more in detail.
The nature-grace motive did not enter Christian
thought before the end of the 12th century, during
the renaissance of the Aristotelian philosophy. It

aimed originally at a religious compromise between the Aristotelian view of nature and the ecclesiastical doctrine of creation, fall into sin, and redemption by Jesus Christ.

The Aristotelian view of nature was no more independent of religious presuppositions than any other philosophical view. It was completely ruled by the dualistic religious basic motive of Greek thought, namely, that of form and matter. Though this terminological denomination is of Aristotelian origin, the central motive designed by it was by no means of Aristotelian invention.

It originated from the meeting between two antagonistic Greek religions, namely, the older nature religion of life and death, and the younger cultural religion of the Olympian gods. Nietzsche and his friend, Rhode, were the first to discover the conflict between these religions in the Greek tragedies. Nietzsche spoke of the contest between the Dionysian and the Apollinian spirit in these tragedies. But in fact here was at issue a conflict in the religious basic motive of the whole Greek life and thought.

The pre-Olympian religion of life and death deified the ever-flowing stream of organic life which originates from mother earth and cannot be fixed or restricted by any corporeal form. It is from this formless stream of life that, in the order of time, the generations of beings separate themselves and appear in an individual bodily shape. This corporeal form can only be maintained at the cost of other living beings, so that the life of the one is the death of the other.

So there is an injustice in any fixed form of life which for this reason must be repaid to the horrible fate of death, designated by the Greek terms *anangkè* and *heimarmenè tuché*. This is the meaning of the mysterious words of the Ionian philosopher of nature, Anaximander: "The divine origin of all things is the *apeiron* (i. e., that which lacks a restricting form). The things return to that from which they originate in conformity to the law of justice. For they pay to each other penalty and retribution for their injustice in the order of time."

Here the central motive of the archaic religion of life and death has found a clear expression in Anaximander's philosophical view of *physis*, or nature. It is the motive of the formless stream of life, ever-flowing throughout the process of becoming and passing away, and pertaining to all perishable things which are born in a corporeal form, and subjected to *anangké*. This is the original sense of the Greek matter-motive. It originated from a deification of the biotic aspect of our temporal horizon of experience and found its most spectacular expression in the cult of Dionysius, imported from Thrace.

The religious form-motive, on the other hand, is the central motive of the younger Olympian religion, the religion of form, measure and harmony, wherein the cultural aspect of the Greek *polis* was deified. It found its most pregnant expression in the Delphian Apollo, the legislator. The Olympian gods are personified cultural powers. They have left mother earth with its everflowing stream of life and its ever-

threatening fate of death, and have acquired the
Olympus as their residence. They have a divine and
immortal, personal form, invisible to the eye of sense,
an ideal form of a splendid beauty, the genuine prototype of the Platonic notion of the metaphysical *eidos,*
or *idea.* But these immortal gods had no power over
the *anangké,* the fate of death of mortals. This is why
the new religion was only accepted as the public
religion of the Greek *polis.* But in their private life
the Greek people held to the old formless deities of
life and death, doubtless more crude and incalculable
than the Olympians, but more efficient as to the
existential needs of man.

Thus the Greek form-matter motive gave expression to a fundamental dualism in the Greek religious
consciousness. As the central starting-point of Greek
philosophy, it was not dependent upon the mythical
forms and representations of the popular belief. By
claiming autonomy over against the latter, Greek
philosophy certainly did not mean to break with the
dualistic basic motive of the Greek religious consciousness. Much rather this motive was the common
starting-point of the different philosophical tendencies and schools. But because of its instrinsically
dualistic character, it drove Greek philosophical
thought into polarly opposed directions. Since a real
synthesis between the opposite motives of form and
matter was not possible, there remained no other
recourse than that of attributing the religious primacy
to one of them with the result that the other was
depreciated. Whereas in the Ionian nature-philosophy

the formless and ever-flowing stream of life was deified, the Aristotelian god is conceived as pure form and the matter-principle is depreciated in the Aristotelian metaphysics as the principle of imperfection.

In the state of apostasy the religious impulse, innate in the human heart, turns away from the living God and is directed towards the temporal horizon of human experience with its diversity of modal aspects. This gives rise to the formation of idols originating in the deification of one of these aspects, i. e., in absolutizing what is only relative. But what is relative can only reveal its meaning in coherence with its correlates. This means that the absolutization of one aspect of our temporal world calls forth, with an inner necessity, correlates of this aspect which now, in the religious consciousness, claim an opposite absoluteness. In other words, every idol gives rise to a counter-idol.

Thus in the Greek religious consciousness the form-motive was bound to the matter-motive as its counterpart. The inner dualism caused in the central starting-point of Greek thought by these two opposite motives gave rise to the dichotomistic view of human nature as a composite of a perishable material body and an immortal, rational soul. It should be noticed that this view originated in the Orphic religious movement. This movement had made the Dionysian religion of life and death into the infra-structure of a higher religion of the celestial sphere, i.e., the starry sky, and interpreted the Olympian religion in this naturalistic sense. In consequence the central motive of form, measure, and harmony was now transferred to the supra-terrestrial sphere of the starry sky. Man was supposed to have a double origin. His rational soul corresponding to the perfect form and harmony of the starry sphere originates in the latter, but his material body originates from the dark and imperfect sphere of mother earth, with its everflowing stream of life and its *anangkē,* its inescapable fate of death. As long as the immortal rational soul is bound to the terrestrial sphere it is obliged to accept a material body as its prison and grave and it must transmigrate from body to body in the everlasting process of becoming, decline, and re-birth.

It is only by means of an ascetic life that the rational soul can purify itself from the contamination with the material body, so that at the end of a long period it may return to its proper home, the celestial sphere of form, measure and harmony.

The great influence of this dualistic Orphic view of human nature upon the Pythagorean school, Empedocles, Parmenides, and Plato, is generally known. Since Parmenides, the founder of Greek metaphysics, this dichotomistic view was combined with the metaphysical opposition between the realm of eternal being, presenting itself in the ideal spherical form of the heaven, and the phenomenal terrestrial world of coming to be and passing away, subjected to the *anangkē.* Plato purified his metaphysics from Parmenides' naturalistic conception of form, and he conceived the eternal forms of being as *eide,* or *ideas,* respectively. In Plato's dialogue, Phaedo, the proof of the immortality of the rational soul is consequently unbreakably bound to the metaphysical doctrine of the eternal ideas as the ideal forms of being. The latter are sharply opposed to the visible world subjected as it is to the matter-principle of becoming and decay. It was supposed that the metaphysical forms of being are only accessible to logico-theoretical thought, viewed as the center of the immortal soul. The logical function of theoretical thought was considered to be completely independent of the material body since it is directed upon the eternal forms of being and must consequently be of the same nature as these imperishable forms. Henceforth the thesis that the logical function of the theoretical act of thought is independent of the material body became a steady argument in the metaphysical proof of the immortality of the rational soul.

But this argument originated in an absolutization of the antithetical relation which is characteristic of the theoretical attitude of thought. We have seen that in this theoretical attitude the logical aspect of our thought is opposed to the non-logical aspects of experience in order to make the latter accessible to a conceptual analysis. In this way we can make the non-logical aspects of our body into the object of our logico-theoretical inquiry. But we have also established that this anti-thetical relation between the logical and the non-logical aspects of our temporal experiential horizon does not correspond to reality. It is only the result of a theoretical abstraction of our logical aspect of thought from its unbreakable bond of coherence with all the other aspects of our experience.

Under the influence of the dualistic religious form-matter motive, however, Greek metaphysics ascribed to this merely theoretical opposition a metaphysical significance, to the effect that the logico-theoretical function of thought was viewed as an independent substance. In this way there arose the idol of the immortal and rational human soul which was identified with the logical function of our act of theoretical thought. In Plato's dialogue, Phaedo, this identification is clearly proclaimed. But it should be noticed that it dated from the first appearance in Greek philosophy of the metaphysical opposition between the eternal form of being and the material world of coming into being and passing away. It was the founder of Greek metaphysics, Parmenides, who was the first to identify theoretical thought with eternal being. In a later phase of his thought, Plato replaced his original view of the simplicity of the human soul by the conception that this soul is composed of two mortal material parts and an immortal spiritual one; nevertheless, he maintained the identification of the latter with the logico-theoretical function of thought. According to him, the latter is the pure form of the soul, viewed apart from its incarnation in the impure material body.

Aristotle, who initially completely accepted both Plato's doctrine of ideas and his dualistic view of soul and body, tried later on to overcome this dualism. He abandoned the Platonic separation between the

world of the ideal forms and the visible world of
perishable material things. He made the ideal forms
into the immanent principles of being in the perishable substances, which are according to him composed
of matter and form. He sought to overcome the central conflict between the matter-motive and the form-
motive in the Greek religious consciousness, by reducing it to the complementary relation of a material
and a form given to it, in the sense in which this
relation is found in the cultural aspect of experience.
As the principle of coming into being and passing
away, matter has, according to him, no actual but
only potential being. It is only by a substantial form
that it can have actual existence. Form and matter
are united in the natural things to one natural substance, and this natural substance would be the
absolute reference point of all properties we ascribe
to the thing.

This metaphysical view was also applied to man
as a natural substance. Thus the rational soul was
conceived as the substantial form of the perishable
material body. Since, however, the soul is only the
substantial form of the body without being itself a
substance, it cannot exist apart from the material
body and lacks, in consequence, immortality. What,
according to Aristotle, is really an immortal substance
is only the active theoretical intellect which, in his
opinion, does not stem from human nature, but comes
from the outside into the soul. This active theoretical
thought, however, lacks any individuality, since individuality stems from matter, and active theoretical

thought remains completely separated from the material body. It is the pure and actual form of thinking, and, as such, it has a general character.

Here the fundamental dualism in the form-matter motive, which at first sight seemed to be overcome by Aristotle, clearly reappears. In fact, it could not be overcome since it ruled the central starting-point of Greek philosophical thought.

Thomas Aquinas tried to accommodate the Aristotelian view of human nature to the doctrine of the Church. First he adapted it to the doctrine of divine creation, which, as such, was incompatible with the Greek form-matter motive. According to Thomas, God created man as a natural substance composed of matter and form. Second, he interpreted the Aristotelian view in such a way that the rational soul was conceived of both as the form of the material body and as an immortal substance which can exist apart from the body. He accepted the Aristotelian view that matter is the principle of individuation and that form as such lacks individuality. The Aristotelian view that the active theoretical intellect does not originate from the natural process of development, but comes from the outside, was interpreted in a so-called psycho-creationist sense. God creates every immortal rational soul apart. But the result of this scholastic accommodation was a complex of insoluble contradictions.

In the first place, the psycho-creationist doctrine contradicts the emphatic biblical statement (Genesis 2:2), that God had finished all his works of creation.

Thus a whole complex of theological pseudo-problems was introduced. If God continues to create rational souls after the fall of man, does he create sinful souls, or should we assume that sin does only originate from the material body? The traditional solution of this problem to the effect that God creates souls deprived of the original state of communion with him, but not sinful in themselves, is unbiblical to such a degree that it does not need any further argumentation. For what else is the fall into sin than breaking the communion with God, i. e., what else than the state of apostasy from him? Secondly, if the immortal soul is individualized only by the material body, how can it retain its individuality after its separation from the body?

I shall not go into a more detailed discussion of these scholastic problems. The *vitium originis* of this psycho-creationist theory is its un-biblical starting-point, which cannot be made innocuous by any scholastic accommodation to the Church's doctrine and by an appeal to texts of Scripture. For the theological exegesis of these texts is in this case itself infected by this un-biblical starting-point. It lacks the *key* of knowledge which alone can open to us the radical sense of the divine Word-revelation. For, let me end with words of Calvin in the beginning of the first chapter of his *Institutio Religionis Christianae*, "The true knowledge of ourselves is dependent upon the true knowledge of God."

What Is Man?

The question, "What is man?" occupies a central place in contemporary European thinking. This question is certainly not new. After every period in the history of Western thought, wherein all interest was concentrated upon the knowledge of the outer world, the immense universe, man began to feel unsatisfied. In this situation human reflection always turns again to the central riddle of man's own existence. As soon as this riddle begins to puzzle human thought, it seems as if the external world recedes from the focus of interest.

In one of his splendid dialogues, Plato pictures his master, Socrates, as a man obsessed with but one aim in his search for wisdom, namely, to know *himself*. As long as I have not succeeded in learning to know myself, said Socrates, I have no time for meddling with other questions that seem to me trifles when compared with this.

In contemporary European thinking, however, the question, "What is man?," is no longer asked from a theoretical viewpoint merely. Much rather it has become a crucial issue for many thinkers because of the spiritual distress of Western society and the fundamental crisis of our culture. It may be that in America this crisis does not occupy the same central place in the reflection of the leading thinkers, as it does in Europe. Nevertheless, America, too, is concerned with the same problem, since it belongs to the sphere of Western civilization.

What, then, is the character of this crisis? And why does the question, "What is man?," today sound like a cry of distress?

The crisis of Western civilization is depicted as a complete decline of human personality, as the rise of the mass-man. This is imputed, by different leading thinkers, to the increasing supremacy of technology, and to the over-organization of modern society. The result, supposedly, is a process of depersonalizing of contemporary life. The modern mass-man has lost all personal traits. His pattern of behavior is prescribed by what is done in general. He shifts the responsibility for his behavior upon an impersonal society. And this society, in turn, seems to be ruled by the robot, the electronic brain, by bureaucracy, fashion, organization and other impersonal powers. As a result, our contemporary society has no room for human personality, and for a real spiritual communion of person with person. Even the family and the church often can no longer guarantee a sphere of personal intercourse. Family life is, to a large degree, dislocated by increasing industrialization. The church itself is confronted with the danger of the depersonalization of congregational life, especially in the big cities.

In addition, the average, secularized man nowadays

has lost any and all true interest in religion. He has fallen prey to a state of spiritual nihilism, i. e., he negates all spiritual values. He has lost all his faith, and denies any higher ideals than the satisfaction of his appetites. Even the Humanistic faith in *mankind,* and in the power of human reason to rule the world and to elevate man to a higher level of freedom and morality, has no longer any appeal to the mind of the present day mass-man. To him God is dead, and the two worlds wars have destroyed the Humanistic ideal of man. This modern man has lost *himself,* and considers himself cast into a world that is meaningless, that offers no hope for a better future.

Western civilization, which displays these terrible symptoms of spiritual decline, finds itself confronted with the totalitarian ideology of Communism. It tries to oppose the latter with the old ideas of democracy, freedom, and of inalienable human rights. But these ideas, too, have been involved in the spiritual crisis, which has sapped their very fundamentals. In earlier times, it is argued, they were rooted both in the Christian faith and in the Humanists's faith in reason. But the increasing relativism, which has affected our Western civilization, has left no room for a strong faith, since it has destroyed the belief in an absolute truth. The traditional faith, which gave man his inspiration, has to a great extent been replaced by technical methods and organization. And in general it is due to such impersonal means that the traditional Christian and the Humanistic traits of our culture are outwardly maintained.

But Western civilization cannot be saved by technical and organizational means alone. The Communistic world-power, whose ideology is still rooted in a strong faith, also has these means at its disposal and has used them very well. Besides, the atom bomb, which terminated the second world war, is no longer an American monopoly. This terrible invention of Western technology can only increase the fear of the impending ruin of our culture. The amazing technical development of Western society, which has produced the modern mass-man, will also destroy our civilization unless a way is found to restore human personality.

It is against this background of spiritual distress that the question: "What is man?" has become truly existential in contemporary European philosophy. It is no longer merely a question of theoretical interest. It has become, rather, a question concerning the whole existence of man in his spiritual anxiety. It is a question of to be or not to be. This also explains the powerful influence of contemporary personalistic and existentialistic philosophical trends upon European literature and upon the youth. Here it is no longer an abstract idealistic image of man as a rational and moral being, which is at issue. Rather, the new philosophical view of man is concerned with man in his concrete situation in the world, with his state of decay as the contemporary mass-man, and with his possibilities of rediscovernig himself as a responsible personality.

This philosophy no longer considers the intellect as the real center of human nature. It has tried to penetrate rather to what it conceived to be the deepest root of human self-hood and the deepest cause of man's spiritual distress. Man is thrown into the world involuntarily. To sustain his life he is obliged to turn to the things that are at hand in his world. The struggle for existence characterizes man's life. But, in this situation of concern, man is in danger of losing himself as a free personality so that he delivers himself to the world. For the human selfhood surpasses all existing things. The human ego is free, it is not at hand as a concrete object. It is able to project its own future, and to say to its past, "I am no longer what I was yesterday. My future is still in my own hand. I can change myself. I can create my future by my own power." But when man reflects on this creative freedom of his selfhood, he is confronted with the deepest cause of his distress, namely, the anxiety and fear of death. Death is here not understood in the merely biological sense, in which it also applies to the animal, but much rather in the sense of the dark nothingness, the night without dawn, which puts an end to all human projects and makes them meaningless. This anxiety, this fear of death is usually suppressed, for such is the mass-man's depersonalized manner of existence. To arrive at a proper, personal existence, man should frankly, and by anticipation, confront himself with death as the nothingness which limits his freedom. He should realize that his freedom is a freedom unto death, ending in the dark nothingness. Thus this first existentialistic approach to human self-knowledge revealed a profoundly pessimistic view of man.

However, other existentialistic thinkers showed a

more hopeful possibility of rediscovering man's true personality. In accordance with the personalistic philosophy of Martin Buber, they pointed to the essential communal relation in our personal life. You and I are correlates, which presuppose each other. I cannot know myself without taking into account that my ego is related to the ego of my fellow-man. And I cannot really have a personal meeting with another ego without love. It is only by such a meeting in love that I can arrive at true self-knowledge and knowledge of my fellow-man.

In this way this philosophy, then, seemed to offer various perspectives for a more profound knowledge of man's selfhood. And there are also many theologians who are of the opinion that this existentialistic approach to the central problem of man's nature and destiny, is of a more biblical character than the traditional theological view of human nature, oriented to ancient Greek philosophy.

I fear that this theological opinion testifies to a lack of self-knowledge in its radical biblical sense. It will presently appear why I think so.

However, let us first establish that the whole preceding diagnosis of the spiritual crisis of Western civilization fails to lay bare the root of the evil. For the symptoms of the spiritual decadence of this civilization, manifesting themselves in an increasing expansion of the nihilistic mind, cannot be explained by external causes.

They are only the ultimate result of a religious process of apostasy, which started with the belief in the absolute self-sufficiency of the rational human personality and was doomed to end with the breaking down of this idol.

How, then, can we arrive at real self-knowledge? The question: "Who is man?" contains a mystery that cannot be explained by man himself.

In the last century, when the belief in the so-called objective science was still predominant in the leading circles, it was supposed that by continued empirical research science would succeed in solving all the problems of human existence. Now there is, doubtless, a scientific way of acquiring knowledge about human existence. There are many special sciences which are concerned with the study of man. But each of them considers human life only from a particular viewpoint or aspect. Physics and chemistry, biology, psychology, historiography, sociology, jurisprudence, ethics, and so forth, they all can furnish interesting information about man. But when one asks them: "What is man himself, in the central unity of his existence, in his selfhood?" then these sciences have no answer. The reason is that they are bound to the temporal order of our experience. Within this temporal order human existence presents a great diversity of aspects, just like the whole temporal world, in which man finds himself placed. Physics and chemistry inform us about the material constellation of the human body, and the electro-magnetic forces operating in it; biology lays bare the functions of our organic life; psychology gives us an insight into the emotional life of feeling and will, and has even penetrated to the unconscious sphere of our mind. History informs us about the development of human culture, linguistics about the human faculty of expressing thoughts and feelings by means of words and other symbolical signs; economics and jurisprudence study the economic and juridical aspects of human social life, and so forth. Thus every special science studies temporal human existence in one of its different aspects.

But all these aspects of our experience and existence within the order of time are related to the central unity of our consciousness, which we call our I, our ego. *I* experience, and *I* exist, and this *I* surpasses the diversity of aspects, which human life displays within the temporal order. The ego is not to be determined by any aspect of our temporal experience, since it is the central reference point of *all* of them. If man would lack this central *I*, he could not have any experience at all.

Consequently, contemporary existentialistic philosophy rightly posited that it is not possible to acquire real self-knowledge by means of scientific research. But it pretended that its own philosophical approach to human existence does lead us to this self-knowledge. Science, so it says, is restricted to the investigation of what is given, to concrete objects at hand. But the human ego is not a given object. It has the freedom to create itself by contriving its own future. Existentialistic philosophy pretends that it is exactly directed upon the discovery of this freedom of the human I, in contrast to all the data at hand in the world.

But is it true that we can arrive at real self-knowledge in this way? Can this philosophy actually penetrate to the real center and root of our existence, as many contemporary theologians think? I am of the opinion that it is a vain illusion to think so.

Philosophical thought is bound to the temporal order of human experience, just as the special sciences are. Within this temporal order man's existence presents itself only in a rich diversity of aspects, but not in that radical and central unity, which we call our I or selfhood. It is true that our temporal existence presents itself as an individual, bodily whole, and that its different aspects are related to this whole, in fact, are only aspects of it. But as a merely temporal wholeness, our human existence does not display that central unity which we are aware of in our self-consciousness.

This central I, which surpasses the temporal order, remains a veritable mystery. As soon as we try to grasp it in a concept or definition, it recedes as a phantom and resolves itself into nothingness. Is it really a nothing, as some philosophers have said?

The mystery of the human I is, that it is, indeed, nothing *in itself;* that is to say, it is nothing as long as we try to conceive it apart from the three central relations which alone give it meaning.

First, our human ego is related to our whole temporal existence and to our entire experience of the temporal world as the central reference point of the latter. Second, it finds itself, indeed, in an essential communal relation to the egos of its fellowmen.

Third, it points beyond itself to its central relation to its divine Origin in Whose image man was created.

The first relation, namely, that of the human ego to the temporal order of the world, in which we are placed, cannot lead us to real self-knowledge, so long as it is viewed in itself alone. The temporal order of human life in the world, with its diversity of aspects, can only turn away our view from the real center of human existence, so long as we seek to know *ourselves* from it. Shall we seek our selfhood in the spatial aspect of our temporal existence, or in the physico-chemical aspect of the material constellation of our body, or in the aspect of its organic life, or in that of emotional feeling? Or should we rather identify our ego with the logical aspect of our thought, or with the historical aspect of our cultural life in a temporal society, or with the aesthetical, or the moral aspect of our temporal existence? By so doing we would lose sight of the real center and radical unity of our human nature. The temporal order of our experiential world is like a prism, which refracts or disperses the sun-light into a rich diversity of colors. None of these colors is the light itself. In the same way the central human ego is not to be determined by any of the different aspects of our temporal, earthly existence.

The second relation, in which our selfhood is to be conceived, is the communal relation of our own ego to that of our fellow-man. This relation can no more lead us to real self-knowledge, than can the relation of our ego to the temporal world, as long as it is viewed in itself alone. The reason is that the ego of our fellow-man confronts us with the same riddle as our own selfhood does. So long as we try to understand the relation between you and me merely from the temporal order of this earthly human existence, we must posit that this relation presents the same diversity of aspects as our own temporal existence. Whether we conceive of it in its moral, psychological, historico-cultural or biological aspects, we will not arrive at any knowledge of the central relationship between your and my selfhood. By so doing we only lose sight of its central character, which surpasses the diversity of aspects in our temporal horizon of existence.

The personalistic and existentialistic views of man have tried to determine the I-thou relation as a relation of love, an inner meeting of the human persons. But within the earthly horizon of time even the love-relations present a diversity of meaning and typical character. Does one refer to the love between husband and wife, or between parents and their children? Or is it the love-relation between fellow-believers, belonging to inter-related churches, that we have in mind? Or is it perhaps the love-relation between compatriots, who have in common the love of their country? Or have we rather in mind the general love of the neighbor in the moral relations of our temporal life? None of these temporal communal relations touch at the central sphere of our selfhood.

And when contemporary philosophy speaks of an inner meeting of the one person with the other, we must ask, "What do you understand by this inner meeting?" A real inner meeting presupposes real self-knowledge, and can only occur in the central religious sphere of our relation with our fellow-man. The temporal love-relations, in the above mentioned typical diversity of meaning, cannot guarantee a true inner meeting. Jesus said, in the Sermon on the Mount, "If ye love them which love you, what thank have ye? for sinners also love those that love them." Jesus here apparently speaks of a love that does not concern the real center of our lives, but only the temporal relations between men in their earthly diversity. But how can we love our enemies and bless those who curse us, and pray for those who persecute us, if we do not love God in Jesus Christ?

Thus the inter-personal relation between you and me cannot lead us to real self-knowledge, as long as it is not conceived in its central sense; and in this central sense it points beyond itself to the ultimate relation between the human I and God. This latter central relation is of a religious character. No philosophical reflection can lead us to real self-knowledge, in a purely philosophical way. The words with which Calvin starts the first chapter of his text-book on the Christian religion: "The true knowledge of ourselves is dependent on the true knowledge of God," are indeed the key to answer the question: "Who is man himself?"

But if that is so, it seems that we should apply to theology for real self-knowledge, since theology seems to be especially concerned with the knowledge of God. However, this too would amount to self-deceit. For as a dogmatical science of the articles of the

Christian faith, theology is no more able to lead us to
real knowledge of ourselves and of God than philosophy or the special sciences which are concerned with
the study of man. This central knowledge can only
be the result of the Word-revelation of God operating in the heart, in the religious center of our existence by the power of the Holy Spirit. Jesus Christ
never blamed the scribes and Pharisees for their lack
of dogmatical theological knowledge. When Herod
asked the Chief priest and scribes where Christ was
to be born, he received an answer that was doubtless
correct from a dogmatical theological viewpoint, since
it was based upon the prophetical texts of the Old
Testament.

Nevertheless, Jesus says that they did not know Him
nor his Father. And how could they have had real
self-knowledge without this knowledge of God in
Jesus Christ?

The traditional theological view of man, which we
find both in Roman Catholic and Protestant scholastic
works on dogmatics, was not at all of a biblical origin.
According to this theological conception of human
nature, man is composed of a mortal, material body
and of an immaterial, rational soul. These components were conceived of as united to one substance.
Nevertheless, according to this view the rational soul
continues to exist as an independent substance after
the separation from the body, i. e., after death. In line
with this view of human nature, man was called a
rational and moral being in contrast to the animal
which lacks a rational soul.

This view of man was, indeed, taken from Greek

philosophy, which sought the center of our human existence in reason, i. e., in the intellect. But in this entire image of man there was no room for the real, i. e., the religious center of our existence which in the Holy Scripture is called our *heart,* the spiritual root of all the temporal manifestations of our life. It was constructed apart from the central theme of the Word-revelation, that of creation, fall into sin, and redemption by Jesus Christ in the communion of the Holy Spirit. And it is this very core of the divine Revelation which alone reveals the true root and center of human life. It is the only key to true self-knowledge in its dependency on the true knowledge of God. It is also the only judge both of all theological and philosophical views of man. As such, this central theme of the Word-revelation cannot be dependent on theological interpretations and conceptions, which are fallible human work, bound to the temporal order of our existence and experience. Its radical sense can only be explained by the Holy Spirit, who opens our *hearts,* so that our belief is no longer a mere acceptance of the articles of the Christian faith, but a living belief, instrumental to the central operation of God's Word in the heart, namely, the religious center of our lives. And this operation does not occur in an individualistic way but in the ecumenical communion of the Holy Spirit who unites all the members of the true Catholic Church in its spiritual sense, irrespective of their temporal denominational divisions.

Naturally, creation, the fall into sin and the redemption through Jesus Christ as the Incarnate Word,

in the communion of the Holy Spirit, are also articles
of faith, which are treated in every theological dogmatics, in addition to other articles which are also,
actually or supposedly, founded in the Holy Scriptures. But in their radical sense as the central theme
of the Word-revelation and the key of knowledge,
they are not merely articles of faith, which are only
the human formulations of the confession of the
Church; much rather, they are the Word of God itself
in its central spiritual power addressing itself to the
heart, the religious core and center of our existence.
In this central confrontation with the Word of God,
man has nothing to give but only to listen and to receive. God does not speak to theologians, philosophers
and scientists, but to sinners, lost in themselves, and
made into His children through the operation of the
Holy Spirit in their hearts. In this central and radical
sense, God's Word, penetrating to the root of our
being, has to become the central motive-power of the
whole of the Christian life within the temporal order
with its rich diversity of aspects, occupational spheres
and tasks. As such, the central theme of creation, fall
into sin and redemption, should also be the central
starting-point and motive power of our theological
and philosophical thought.

Is it necessary, at this point, to consider the radical
meaning of this central theme of the divine Word-
Revelation? Is it not rather well known to all of us
since the beginning of our Christian education?

It may well be questioned whether this is really
true. I am afraid that many Christians have only a

theological knowledge of creation, fall into sin and redemption by Jesus Christ, and, that this central theme of the Word-Revelation has not yet become the central motive-power of their lives.

What is the radical, biblical sense of the revelation of creation? As Creator, God reveals Himself as the absolute Origin of all that exists outside of Himself. There is no power in the world that is independent of Him. Even Satan is a creature and his power is taken from creation, namely, from the creation of man in the image of God. If man had not been created in God's image, Satan's suggestion that man would be like God would have had no single power over the human heart. He could only give this power an apostate direction, but his power does not originate from himself. If our heart finds itself fully in the grip of the self-revelation of God as Creator, we can no longer imagine that there would exist a safe and neutral zone which is withdrawn from God. This is the fundamental difference between the living God and the idols which originate from an absolutization of what has only a relative and dependent existence. The ancient Greeks, whose conception of human nature had such a predominant influence upon the traditional theological view of man, worshipped their Olympian gods, who were merely deified cultural powers of Greek society. These gods were represented as invisible and immortal beings endowed with a splendid beauty and a supra-human power. But these splendid gods had no power over the fate of death, to which mortals are subjected. This is why the famous

Greek poet, Homer, said: "Even the immortal gods cannot help lamentable man, when the horrible fate of death strikes him down." And the same poet says that the immortal gods fight shy of every contact with the realm of death.

But hear now what Psalm one hundred and thirty-nine says about God: "Whither shall I go from thy Spirit? Or whither shall I flee from thy presence? If I ascend up into heaven, thou art there: If I make my bed in the realm of death, behold, thou art there." Here we face the living God, as Creator, whom the ancient Greeks did not know.

In an indissoluble contact with this self-revelation as Creator, God has revealed man to himself. Man was created in the image of God. Just as God is the absolute Origin of all that exists outside of Himself, so He created man as a being, in whom the entire diversity of aspects and faculties of the temporal world is concentrated within the religious center of his existence, which we call our I, and which the Holy Scripture calls our *heart,* in a pregnant, religious sense. As the central seat of the image of God, the human selfhood was endowed with the innate religious impulse to concentrate his whole temporal life and the whole temporal world upon the service of love to God. And since the love for God implies the love for His image in man, the whole diversity of temporal ordinances of God is related to the central, religious commandment of love, namely, "thou shalt love the Lord, thy God, with all thy heart, soul and mind, and thy neighbor as thyself." This is the radical biblical sense of the creation of man in the image of God. It leaves no room for any neutral sphere in life, which could be withdrawn from the central commandment in the kingdom of God.

Since the image of God in man concerned the radix, that is, the religious center and root of our entire temporal existence, it follows that the fall into sin can only be understood in the same radical, biblical sense. The entire fall into sin can be summed up as a false illusion, which arose in the human heart, namely, that the human I has the same absolute existence as God Himself. This was the false insinuation of Satan, to which man gave ear: "Ye shall be like God." This apostasy from the living God implied the spiritual death of man, since the human I is nothing in itself and can only live from the Word of God and in the love-communion with its divine Creator. However, this original sin could not destroy the religious center of human existence with its innate religious impulse to seek for its absolute Origin. It could only lead this central impulsion in a false, apostate direction by diverting it to the temporal world with its rich diversity of aspects, which, however, have only a relative sense.

By seeking his God and himself in the temporal world, and by elevating a relative and dependent aspect of this world to the rank of the absolute, man fell a prey to idolatry. He lost the true knowledge of God and true self-knowledge. The idea that true self-knowledge may be regained by an existentialistic philosophy, apart from the divine Word-revelation, is nothing but the old vain illusion that the human I is something in itself, independent of God who has revealed Himself as the Creator.

It is only in Jesus Christ, the incarnate Word and Redeemer, that the image of God has been restored in the religious center of human nature. The redemption by Jesus Christ in its radical biblical sense, means the rebirth of our *heart* and must reveal itself in the whole of our temporal life. Consequently, there now can be no real self-knowledge apart from Jesus Christ. And this biblical self-knowledge implies that our whole world-and-life-view must be reformed in a Christo-centric sense; so that every dualistic view of common grace which separates the latter from its true religious root and center in Jesus Christ should be rejected in principle.

The history of dogmatic theology proves that it is possible to give an apparently orthodox theoretical explanation of the articles of faith pertaining to the threefold central theme of the Holy Scripture, without any awareness of the central and radical significance of the latter for the view of human nature and of the temporal world. In this case theological thought does not really find itself in the grip of the Word of God. The latter has not become its central basic motive, its central impelling force. Rather, it proves to be influenced by another, a non-biblical central motive, which gives to it its ultimate direction.

Such was the scholastic theme of nature and grace (introduced into Roman Catholic theology and philosophy since the 13th century) which ruled the traditional theological view of man. It led scholastic theology to divide human life into two spheres, namely, the natural and the supra-natural. Human nature was supposed to belong to the natural sphere, and was supposed to find its center in natural reason. This human reason would be able to acquire a right insight into human nature, and into all other so-called natural truths, apart from any divine Revelation, by its own natural light alone.

Of course, it was granted that this rational nature of man was created by God. But this theological acceptance of creation as revealed truth did not influence the view of human nature itself. This view was much rather ruled by the dualistic pagan religious basic motive of Greek thought, which led to a so-called dichotomistic conception of the nature of man.

In addition to his rational-ethical nature, man was supposed to have been endowed with a supra-natural gift of grace, namely, participation in the divine nature. According to Roman Catholic doctrine this supra-natural gift of grace was lost by the fall into sin. It is regained by the supra-natural means of grace, which Christ has entrusted to his Church. In this way, the human rational nature would be elevated to that supra-natural state of perfection to which it was destined after the plan of creation. It was, however, granted that man cannot arrive at this state without faith, which is itself a gift of grace to the human intellect; it is, therefore, only by faith that we can accept the supra-natural truths of divine Revelation. But the supra-natural sphere of grace presupposes the natural sphere of human life, namely, human nature. This nature, according to the Roman Catholic view, was not radically corrupted by sin; it was only wounded, since, after the plan of creation, it was destined to be united with the supra-natural gift of grace. As a result of original sin, human nature lost its original harmony. The sensuous inclinations are in opposition to natural reason which should rule over them. Nevertheless, man can arrive at the acquisition of natural virtues by which the rule of reason over the sensuous inclinations is realized. Only the supra-natural virtues of faith, hope and Christian love belong to the sphere of grace.

This is the view of human nature which has been sanctioned by the doctrine of the Roman Catholic Church. It has completely abandoned the *radical* sense of creation, fall and redemption, as they are revealed to us in the Word of God.

The Roman Catholic view of this central theme of Revelation was rejected by the Reformation. But how is it to be explained that the conception of human nature as a composite of a material body and an immortal, rational soul was, nevertheless, generally accepted by both scholastic Lutheran and Reformed theology. Was this conception not taken from Greek philosophy, whose pagan religious basic motive was radically opposed to that of Holy Scripture? Did this Roman dualism not fail to evaluate the biblical insight into the religious root and center of human existence? Was it, consequently, not incompatible with the biblical doctrine concerning the radical character of the fall into sin, which affected human nature in its very root?

How, then, could this un-biblical view of man be maintained? The reason is that the scholastic basic motive of nature and grace of Roman Catholicism continued to influence the theological and philosophical views of the Reformation. This motive introduced a dualism into the entire view of man and the world, which could not fail to withdraw Christian thought from the radical and integral grip of the Word of God.

It is this very dualism which testifies to its un-biblical character. It was the result of the attempt to accommodate the Greek view of nature to the biblical doctrine of grace. In fact, this scholastic motive of accommodation resulted in a radical deformation of the central theme of the Word-revelation. The scholastic view that created human nature finds its center in an autonomous human reason cannot be accommodated to the radical biblical view of creation. It implied that in the natural sphere of life man would be independent of the Word of God. This false division of human life into a natural and a supra-natural sphere became the starting-point of the process of secularization, which resulted in the crisis of Western culture, in its spiritual uprooting. In fact, it abandoned the so-called natural sphere to the rule of the apostate religious basic motive, initially to that of Greek thought, later on to that of modern Humanism.

Human reason is not an independent substance; much rather it is an instrument. The *I* is the hidden player, who avails himself of it.

And the central motive that rules both human thought and the human ego itself, is of a central religious nature.

The question: "What is man? Who is he?", cannot be answered by man himself. But it has been answered by God's Word-revelation, which uncovers the religious root and center of human nature in its creation, fall into sin and redemption by Jesus Christ. Man lost true self-knowledge since he lost the true knowledge of God. But all idols of the human selfhood, which man in his apostasy has devised, break down when they are confronted with the Word of God, which unmasks their vanity and nothingness. It is this Word alone, which by its radical grip can bring about a real reformation of our view of man and of our view of the temporal world; and such an inner reformation is the very opposite of the scholastic device of accommodation.

THE AUTHOR

Dr. Herman Dooyeweerd has been professor of Law in the Free University of Amsterdam since 1926. He is the founder of the new school of Christian philosophy — "The Philosophy of the Cosmonomic Idea" — which has attracted so much attention on the Continent. Since the translation of Dooyeweerd's *A New Critique of Theoretical Thought* (four volumes) in 1957 and his extensive lecture tour through the United States and Canada in 1959, his philosophy has aroused more and more interest in America.

The author of many works in the fields of philosophy and jurisprudence, he has in addition held many posts of a public nature in the Netherlands. For many years he was executive secretary of the Dr. Abraham Kuyper Foundation at the Hague, and as such established its quarterly *Antirevolutionaire Staatkunde*. He is a Fellow of the Royal Dutch Academy of Sciences.

In addition to the University of Amsterdam, the Universities of Utrecht, Leiden, and Groningen; the Technical School of Delft and the School of Economics at Rotterdam all have special chairs of philosophy held by members of this new school. Its leading members include Dr. D. H. Vollenhoven of the Netherlands, Dr. H. G. Stoker of South Africa, and Dr. Cornelius Van Til of this country.

Originally published in 1960 *The Twilight of Western Thought* has been revised for publication in the University Series (*Philosophical Studies*) of The Craig Press.